MW00559334

THREE CHAN (ZEN) CLASSICS

BDK English Tripiṭaka 74-I, II, III

THREE CHAN CLASSICS

The Recorded Sayings of Linji

Wumen's Gate

The Faith-Mind Maxim

Taishō Volumes 47 and 48
Numbers 1985, 2005, 2010

Numata Center
for Buddhist Translation and Research
1999

First Printing, 1999
ISBN: 1-886439-07-9
Library of Congress Catalog Card Number: 97-069167

Published by
Numata Center for Buddhist Translation and Research
2620 Warring Street
Berkeley, California 94704

Printed in the United States of America

A Message on the Publication of the English Tripiṭaka

The Buddhist canon is said to contain eighty-four thousand different teachings. I believe that this is because the Buddha's basic approach was to prescribe a different treatment for every spiritual ailment, much as a doctor prescribes a different medicine for every medical ailment. Thus his teachings were always appropriate for the particular suffering individual and for the time at which the teaching was given, and over the ages not one of his prescriptions has failed to relieve the suffering to which it was addressed.

Ever since the Buddha's Great Demise over twenty-five hundred years ago, his message of wisdom and compassion has spread throughout the world. Yet no one has ever attempted to translate the entire Buddhist canon into English throughout the history of Japan. It is my greatest wish to see this done and to make the translations available to the many English-speaking people who have never had the opportunity to learn about the Buddha's teachings.

Of course, it would be impossible to translate all of the Buddha's eighty-four thousand teachings in a few years. I have, therefore, had one hundred thirty-nine of the scriptural texts in the prodigious Taishō edition of the Chinese Buddhist canon selected for inclusion in the First Series of this translation project.

It is in the nature of this undertaking that the results are bound to be criticized. Nonetheless, I am convinced that unless someone takes it upon himself or herself to initiate this project, it will never be done. At the same time, I hope that an improved, revised edition will appear in the future.

It is most gratifying that, thanks to the efforts of more than a hundred Buddhist scholars from the East and the West, this monumental project has finally gotten off the ground. May the rays of the Wisdom of the Compassionate One reach each and every person in the world.

NUMATA Yehan
Founder of the English
Tripiṭaka Project

August 7, 1991

Editorial Foreword

In January, 1982, Dr. NUMATA Yehan, the founder of the Bukkyō Dendō Kyōkai (Society for the Promotion of Buddhism), decided to begin the monumental task of translating the complete Taishō edition of the Chinese Tripiṭaka (Buddhist Canon) into the English language. Under his leadership, a special preparatory committee was organized in April, 1982. By July of the same year, the Translation Committee of the English Tripiṭaka was officially convened.

The initial Committee consisted of the following members: HANAYAMA Shōyū (Chairperson); BANDŌ Shōjun; ISHIGAMI Zennō; KAMATA Shigeo; KANAOKA Shūyū; MAYEDA Sengaku; NARA Yasuaki; SAYEKI Shinkō; (late) SHIOIRI Ryōtatsu; TAMARU Noriyoshi; (late) TAMURA Kwansei; URYŪZU Ryūshin; and YUYAMA Akira. Assistant members of the Committee were as follows: KANAZAWA Atsushi; WATANABE Shōgo; Rolf Giebel of New Zealand; and Rudy Smet of Belgium.

After holding planning meetings on a monthly basis, the Committee selected 139 texts for the First Series of translations, an estimated one hundred printed volumes in all. The texts selected are not necessarily limited to those originally written in India but also include works written or composed in China and Japan. While the publication of the First Series proceeds, the texts for the Second Series will be selected from among the remaining works; this process will continue until all the texts, in Japanese as well as in Chinese, have been published.

Frankly speaking, it will take perhaps one hundred years or more to accomplish the English translation of the complete Chinese and Japanese texts, for they consist of thousands of works. Nevertheless, as Dr. NUMATA wished, it is the sincere hope of the Committee that this project will continue unto completion, even after all its present members have passed away.

It must be mentioned here that the final object of this project is not academic fulfillment but the transmission of the teaching of the

Buddha to the whole world in order to create harmony and peace among mankind. Therefore, any notes, such as footnotes and endnotes, which might be indispensable for academic purposes, are not given in the English translations, since they might make the general reader lose interest in the Buddhist scriptures. Instead, a glossary is added at the end of each work, in accordance with the translators' wish.

To my great regret, however, Dr. NUMATA passed away on May 5, 1994, at the age of 97, entrusting his son, Mr. NUMATA Toshihide, with the continuation and completion of the Translation Project. The Committee also lost its able and devoted Chairperson, Professor HANAYAMA Shōyū, on June 16, 1995, at the age of 63. After these severe blows, the Committee elected me, Vice-President of the Musashino Women's College, to be the Chair in October, 1995. The Committee has renewed its determination to carry out the noble intention of Dr. NUMATA, under the leadership of Mr. NUMATA Toshihide.

The present members of the Committee are MAYEDA Sengaku (Chairperson), BANDŌ Shōjun, ISHIGAMI Zennō, ICHISHIMA Shōshin, KAMATA Shigeo, KANAOKA Shūyū, NARA Yasuaki, SAYEKI Shinkō, TAMARU Noriyoshi, URYŪZU Ryūshin, and YUYAMA Akira. Assistant members are WATANABE Shōgo and MINOWA Kenryō.

The Numata Center for Buddhist Translation and Research was established in November, 1984, in Berkeley, California, U.S.A., to assist in the publication of the BDK English Tripiṭaka First Series. In December, 1991, the Publication Committee was organized at the Numata Center, with Professor Philip Yampolsky as the Chairperson. To our sorrow, Professor Yampolsky passed away in July, 1996, but thankfully Dr. Kenneth Inada is continuing the work as Chairperson. The Numata Center has thus far published eleven volumes and has been distributing them. All of the remaining texts will be published under the supervision of this Committee, in close cooperation with the Translation Committee in Tokyo.

MAYEDA Sengaku
Chairperson
Translation Committee of
the BDK English Tripiṭaka

June 1, 1997

Publisher's Foreword

The Publication Committee works in close cooperation with the Editorial Committee of the BDK English Tripiṭaka in Tokyo, Japan. Since December 1991, it has operated from the Numata Center for Buddhist Translation and Research in Berkeley, California. Its principal mission is to oversee and facilitate the publication in English of selected texts from the one hundred-volume Taishō Edition of the Chinese Tripiṭaka, along with a few major influential Japanese Buddhist texts not in the Tripiṭaka. The list of selected texts is conveniently appended at the end of each volume. In the text itself, the Taishō Edition page and column designations are provided in the margins.

The Committee is committed to the task of publishing clear, readable English texts. It honors the deep faith, spirit, and concern of the late Reverend Doctor NUMATA Yehan to disseminate Buddhist teachings throughout the world.

In July 1996, the Committee unfortunately lost its valued Chairperson, Dr. Philip Yampolsky, who was a stalwart leader, trusted friend, and esteemed colleague. We follow in his shadow. In February 1997, I was appointed to guide the Committee in his place.

The Committee is charged with the normal duties of a publishing firm—general editing, formatting, copyediting, proofreading, indexing, and checking linguistic fidelity. The Committee members are Diane Ames, Brian Galloway, Nobuo Haneda, Charles Niimi, Koh Nishiike, and the president and director of the Numata Center, Reverend Kiyoshi S. Yamashita.

Kenneth K. Inada
Chairperson
Publication Committee

June 1, 1997

Contents

The Recorded Sayings of Linji

Translated from the Chinese
Taishō Volume 47, Number 1985

by

J. C. Cleary

Translator's Introduction

The Recorded Sayings of Linji (in Chinese *Linji Lu*, in Japanese *Rinzai Roku*) is one of the seminal books of Zen. The great Zen teacher Linji lived and worked in ninth century China, but his teachings continued to guide and influence people for centuries afterwards, and he was considered the grand ancestor of major streams of Zen in China, Korea, Vietnam, and Japan. The direct, incisive teachings preserved in his recorded sayings have shown a perennial power to challenge and stimulate would-be seekers of the truth. Thus for more than a millenium, the *Recorded Sayings of Linji* has served as one of the classic works of Great Vehicle Buddhism in the Far East.

The modern reader will surely be struck by the very "modernity" of these thousand year old teachings. Linji strips away the supernatural aura of the buddhas and bodhisattvas, and refers the symbolism of the Buddhist scriptures to human processes, to actual and potential psychological transformations involving individuals and social groups. He analyses the relationship of language to reality and of conditioning to perception and motivation in ways that both prefigure and surpass "modern" discussions on these points.

Linji insists to his listeners that the concepts and imagery of the Buddhist Teachings refer to possibilities within us, and are meant to be applied by present day people in the context of real life, day to day and moment to moment. No concepts are made sacrosanct, no procedures idolized. The Buddhist Teachings are seen as provisional methods adopted to enable people to break free from their conditioning and habit patterns. Genuine teachers can lead sincere students to recognize Reality, and thereby open the way for them to actualize the wisdom and compassion inherent in their real identity, their buddha-nature.

In Linji's Zen as in all Great Vehicle Buddhism, correct insight into the emptiness of all things is inseparable from an active life of compassion in response to the needs of other beings. This is related not as a paradox, but as a factual description of the Path by the travellers.

Linji's blunt and plainspoken style brings Buddhism down to earth, into our own intimate consciousness, and introduces a vast, subtle all-encompassing form of perception. Linji's teachings have crossed many barriers of place and time before now. Whether or not they are already familiar with Zen Buddhism, modern readers can read Linji's sayings as a direct demonstration of its viewpoint and call.

Prefaces

Linquan's Preface of 1297

The streams branching off from [the Sixth Zen Patriarch Huineng 495a03
of] Caoqi have welled up and flowed onward without end. The branch coming through [Huineng's immediate disciple Huairang of] Nanyue has been lofty, continuing without end. Clouds overspread it, and its branches and leaves have grown luxuriantly. Not only does it provide shade for humans and devas, but it also displays the Path of the Ancestral Teachers.

For explanations without explanations, one must know that the meaning is not in the words. If one hears without hearing, one is certain after all that the words do not contain the meaning. This is the indescribable Path that is the ultimate truth: the rest are mere shadows and echoes.

Thus the ancestral teacher Linji used the eye of the Correct Dharma to illuminate the Mind of Nirvana. With great wisdom and great compassion, he activated great potential and great function. With blows and shouts he cut off worldly sentiments. Like a lightning bolt or a shooting star, he was difficult to make contact with. How could he allow you time to ponder or think back? Not only has the cock already flown past Silla: [by thinking and pondering] you want to send a phoenix to overtake the Milky Way.

[Linji] did not leave any tracks: he crossed through the Mystic Barrier, to enable all deluded beings in the triple world to return to the One True Reality. All the brave people under heaven look up to him with respect. To be the ancestral teacher of a whole school, this is the way he had to be.

The present imperially appointed chief monk, Zen master Xuetang, is an eighteenth generation descendant of Linji. The recorded sayings of Linji are found everywhere in north and south

China. I happened to obtain this text when I was in Yuhang. It was finding a jewel for a pauper, like finding a light in the dark. I was leaping and shouting with joy: I was irresistibly moved and stimulated.

Subsequently I endowed a perpetual fund [to provide for] the printing and circulation [of the *Recorded Sayings of Linji*] so that they can be distributed to the temples. Such a wondrous thing as this is indeed "hard to encounter even in a thousand years." Ah!

> The sound of gold scattered on the ground is heard all over the country.
> We know for certain the price of the jewel is hard to repay.

[Dated and signed] Second year of the Yuan Zhen era [1297 A.D.], ding-wei in the cycle of years. Abbot of Baoen Zen Temple, heir to the patriarchs, having washed his hands and burned incense, carefully writes this.

Preface of the Censor Guo Tianxi [1298 A.D.]

The Lord Buddha entrusted the treasury of the True Dharma Eye, the Wondrous Mind of Nirvana, to Mahākāśyapa. He was the first patriarch [of Zen in India]. It was passed down until it reached the twenty-eighth patriarch Bodhidharma, who came to China with the esoteric seal of all the buddhas of past, present, and future in all directions. This is when China first began to realize that there is a
495b special transmission outside the scriptural teachings: "Without establishing words [as sacred], directly pointing to the human mind, to enable people to see their real nature and become enlightened."

After this, the udumbara flower [symbolic of the enlightened ones] appeared in due time, fragrant and lush: one flower [the patriarchal transmission] opened into five petals [the Five Houses of Zen]. Their perfumed wind circles the earth and their precious color lights up the sky. Each emits an infinite light which shines on a galaxy of worlds.

Amidst this, there was a great bhikṣu [Linji] who for the sake of the one great matter stayed on Huangbo Mountain. Three times he asked for instructions [from Zen teacher Huangbo], and three times he was beaten. Later he went to old man Dayu's place on the riverbank at Gaoan: only then was Linji totally sealed and approved. His whole life he used the diamond king's jewel sword: when he met ordinary people, he slew them, and when he met sages, he slew them. When the wind moves, the grass bends over: the command prevails everywhere.

Linji is like a snow-white elephant king, like a golden-haired lion. When he crouches to spring and roars, the hearts and brains of jackals and wild foxes burst. When the animals see him, they all tremble. He is like a tremendous wave, like a fearsome cliff: he stands like a wall ten thousand fathoms high. He makes those on the road dare not take a step for fear of losing their lives.

Even those who have [been forged] by the hammer and tongs of an experienced adept will break into a sweat when they see Linji. His "Three Mysteries" and "Three Essentials", his removing the scene and removing the person: these are words of gold and jade. They are like wind-tested masts, like battle-tested warhorses. They are fast as lightning and thunder. Like crushing waves, they flood through all the strongholds, and shatter the enemy battlelines.

Heaven turns and earth revolves as Linji moves freely in all directions. He has almost cut off all the other streams, so that all over the world all Zen students scatter before his wind. Thus his gate is high and remote and unbending and hard to enter. In general, the work of wondrous function [such as Linji's] is not within words, nor is it apart from words. Those for whom the whole world is an eye can recognize it. At the end, [Linji died with these words to his successor:] "The treasury of my True Dharma Eye will be destroyed by this blind donkey!"

Linji's appearance in the world is fully recorded in books like the *Transmission of the Lamp*: I shall not repeat it here. From [his successor] Master Jiang of Xinghua on down, his descendants have stretched out like clouds and spread and flourished. Among them have been many people of great capacity, people who radiate down upon the mountains and rivers, outshining ancient and modern. Everywhere throughout the Zen communities they have transformed ordinary practices and spoken of the Real. They have reapplied guidelines and standards and shown the eloquence of enlightened ones, opening teaching halls and expounding the Dharma for people.

For example, [there were] Master Yuan of Ciming and Master Jue of Langlang: both were Great Dharma Kings and teachers of humans and devas. At present, the great teacher Xuetang is the legitimate eighteenth generation descendant of Linji, the tenth generation of Langlang's stream. [Linji's descendants] have been respected by kings and their ministers, and received honor and renown among both monks and nuns and laypeople. They are also the [outstanding exemplars], the dragons and elephants among the Buddhist community.

Those who did not forget the benevolence and virtue of the ancestral teachers have always been afraid that Linji's every word and phrase, his blows and shouts, his lessons and teachings, his recorded sayings, would not be widely known. [Therefore] they have had them printed and circulated, drawing on the resources of the Zen communities, and have asked [me] Guo Tianxi, the Layman of North Mountain, to compose a preface for it.

I salute [my teacher] Master Xuetang: he has carried out the
things that have always been hard for the ancestral teachers to do.
495c When it comes to honoring his departed ancestors, acknowledging
their benevolence and repaying it, he is not lacking in this. He has
taken a cud spit up by a five-hundred-year-old madman, picked it
up again, and offered it to you. Will the present generation of patch-
robed monks be willing to chew it up fine and savor it?

The pearl brought back from Hepu is special indeed, but there's nothing wrong either with the kernel popping in the cold ashes.

[Dated and signed] Second year of the Da De era [1298 A.D.], eighth month. The Censor Guo Tianxi burns incense, bows nine times, and writes this.

Preface by Wufeng Puxiu

Linji thought Huangbo Mountain was lofty, so he dared to confront and capture the tiger there [Zen master Huangbo]. The shore of buddhahood is far away, but he was able to steer his boat following the current [that leads there]. When he showed poisonous teeth and claws, these were still methods of kind compassion. With a slap on the cheek [from Huangbo], Linji avoided the trouble of sinking his teeth in and smearing his lips. Three punches [from Linji] to the ribs [of Dayu]: one could say he poured out his heart and guts.

The Three Mysteries are in his hand, the seven aids to enlightenment accompany his person. Touch him and the rocks shatter and the cliffs tumble. Try to form an opinion of him, and thunder rumbles and lightning flashes. His front gate is solitary and steep; his inner sanctum is vast and deep. We can only look from afar on his cliff: we cannot approach.

Here [we salute] the imperially appointed chief monk Master Xuetang: those who can sympathize with and appreciate such rare fine music are bound to be few. He has wished to print and to put into wide circulation old texts of the recorded sayings [of Zen masters] that are rarely seen [nowadays] in the Zen communities. While [thus] seeking out true Buddhists, he has revived this literature, to enable people to come in contact with its mysteries and gain the use of them. Thus does Xuetang propagate the Path of the ancestral teachers of Zen and bestow blessings on later generations.

[Linji's teaching methods,] his blows and shouts, his explaining clearly in the light of sparks struck from stone or a flash of lightning, raising the issue straight on or from the side, requiring people to observe their eyebrows and nostrils, and other devices are set down in previous records: no need to repeat here.

Ah! From the ancestral teacher Linji the transmission went through six generations, coming to the great Zen teacher Fenyang [947–1024]. Six venerable adepts have come forth like heroes in Fenyang's line [through his immediate disciples] Yuan of Ciming and Jue of Langlang.

Yuan transmitted it to Hui of Yangqi, who transmitted it to
Duan of Baiyun, who transmitted it to Yan of Wuzu. Yan transmitted it to [three great disciples, known as] Foguo, Fojian, and Qi of
Tianmu. Foguo transmitted it to Long of Tiger Hill and to Dahui
Gao. Long transmitted it to Hua of Yingyan. Hua transmitted it to
Jie of Miyan. Jie transmitted it to Yue of Songyuan. Yue transmitted it to Tong of Wude. Tong transmitted it to Du of Xuzhou. Du
transmitted it to Fu of Tiger Cliff on Mt. Jingshan. Qi of Tianmu
transmitted it to He of Ruzhou. He transmitted it to Bao of Zhulin,
who transmitted it to An of Zhulin, who transmitted it to Hai of
496a Zhulin. Hai transmitted it to Zhang of Qingshou, Yi of Bairun, and
Xuan of Guiyun. Xuan transmitted it to Liang of Pingshan. Yi of
Bairun transmitted it to Fang of Chongxu and Gui of Laimu. Zhang
of Qingshou transmitted it to the Great Teacher of Haiyun and to Yi
of Zhulin. Yi transmitted it to Hui of Longhua. Haiyun transmitted
it to Lang of Keyan, Yu of Longgong, and Xuan of Yiyan. Lang of
Keyan transmitted it to Mr. Liu Wenzhen of Taifu and the Man of
Qingshou. Yu of Longgong transmitted it to Hai of Daming. Xuan of
Yiyan transmitted it to An of Qingshou.

[Six generations after Linji, Fenyang's great disciple] Jue of Langlang transmitted it to Yue of Letan, who transmitted it to Zhen of Biling, who transmitted it to Bai of Baishui, who transmitted it to Dang of Tianning, who transmitted it to Chun of Cizhao, who transmitted it to Bao of Zhengzhou. Bao transmitted it to Zang of Zhulin, Heng of Qingshou, and Jian of Shaolin. Heng of Qingshou transmitted it to Bian of Dongping and Zhao of Dayuan. Jian of Shaolin transmitted it to Tong of Fawang, who transmitted it to Jue of Anxian, who transmitted it to Zhi of Nanjing and Zan of Xi-an. Zhi of Nanjing transmitted it to Zhan of Shoufeng. Zan of Xi-an transmitted it to Ren of Xuetang. Thus Xuetang is an eighteenth generation descendant of Linji.

All of [the Zen masters listed above] had gates that were solitary and steep, and mastery of teaching devices that went freely in all directions. All were descendants fully capable of taking charge of the family. The flame has been perpetuated from lamp to lamp up until today. This is the meaning of the saying "When the source is pure, the stream is long."

Zen master Xuetang is my "grandfather" [in the transmission]: he has directed me to compose a preface and I have happily written one. Those whose cheeks can be seen from the back of their heads and who have the eye on their foreheads will give a great laugh.

[Here] in the Retirement Hall of Kaitai Temple, I, Puxiu of Wufeng, the twentieth generation descendant and successor of the ancestral teacher [Linji], perform ablutions after a vegetarian feast, burn incense, and bow in homage as I write this.

Preface Composed by Ma Fang [1120 A.D.]

Who was Scholar of the Yankang Palace, Court Grandee of Gold and Purple Light, Pacification Commissioner of Zhending Circuit, and Commander in Chief of the Cavalry and Infantry, and concurrently Supervisor of Chengde Military District.

On Huangbo Mountain, [Linji] encountered painful beatings; it was on Dayu's ribs that he finally knew how to plant his fists. "Talkative old granny!" "Bed-wetting devil!" "This crazy guy again plucks the tiger's whiskers!" Planting pine trees in the mountain valleys, as a signpost for later generations. When he broke the earth with his hoe, how many were buried alive? He let a younger disciple slap him across the mouth. He said goodbye and burned the lectern. He cut off all tongues. "If it's not south of the river, it's north of the river." His abode looked out upon an ancient ford, and he extended aid to those coming and going. He held fast the essential crossing place, towering up like a wall ten thousand fathoms high. Taking away the person, taking away the scene, he molded immortals. With his "Three Essentials" and "Three Mysteries", he forged patch-robed ones. He was always at home, but never away from the middle of the road. "The true person without position, goes in and out through your face." When the two 496b groups of monks both shouted at once, guest and host were clear. "Perceiving and functioning at the same time, fundamentally there is no before and after." The water chestnut flowers faced his form, the empty valley transmitted his voice. His subtle responses had no location: he left no tracks or traces. Brushing his robe along as he moved south, he left behind a great reputation. Xinghua served him as a pupil does a teacher, and Dongtang respectfully attended upon him. With but a brass pitcher and an iron bowl, he shut his door and cut off all words. He lived to grow old at leisure among the cloudy pines, expansive and satisfied.

Once as he sat facing the wall, after a while he tacitly indicated that he was about to die. When asked to whom he would transmit the Correct Dharma, [Linji said:] "It perishes with this blind donkey," [referring to his successor Xinghua.]

Old man Yan of Yuanjue has checked out [this copy] for present circulation, so there are no errors or spurious additions.

There is just one more shout that we still must discuss. I hope Zen people with eyes will not be adverse to bringing it up.

[Dated] Xuan He era, geng-zi year [1120 A.D.], mid-autumn day. I dutifully compose a preface.

The Recorded Sayings of Zen Master Linji

The local officials invited Linji to preach. Linji went up to the teaching hall and said: "Today I have no alternative but to bend to human sentiment—thus I have ascended to this seat [to preach]. By the standards of the Zen school, when you attempt to extol the great matter [of enlightenment], you simply cannot open your mouth. There's no place for you to get a foothold. Today I have been insisitently invited by the chief official in the area—how could I not reveal the guiding principles of Zen? Is there anyone here who is an expert general, who can extend his battle lines and unfurl his flags right away? Show us some proof so we can see."

A monk asked: "What is the main meaning of the Buddha Dharma?" Linji gave a shout. The monk bowed. Linji said: "This monk, however, only knows the theory of it."

A monk asked: "Whose family song do you sing? Whose successor are you in your Zen style?"

Linji said: "When I was at Huangbo's place, three times I asked, and three times I was beaten."

The monk hesitated, trying to think of what to say. Linji then shouted at him, hit him, and said: "You cannot drive nails into empty space."

There was a lecturer-monk who asked: "Surely the scriptural teachings of the three vehicles make clear what buddha-nature is, do they not?"

Linji said: "The wild weeds have never been chopped down."

The lecturer said: "How could Buddha deceive people?"

Linji said: "Where is Buddha?"

The lecturer could say nothing.

Linji said: "Here in front of this honored official you have tried to deceive me. Go away now—you are preventing other people from asking their questions."

Then Linji continued: "Today's Dharma assembly is for the sake of the one great matter [of opening up your enlightened perception]. Are there any other questioners? Please pose your questions quickly.

"As soon as you open your mouths, it already has nothing to do with it. Why so? Haven't you read what Śākyamuni Buddha said: 'The Dharma is detached from language, because it is not in the province of causes and conditions.' Because you cannot fully believe
496c this, today [I give you] these creeping vines [of verbal explanation]. I'm afraid I will make all you officials get stuck [somewhere in the explanation], so you stay ignorant of your buddha-nature. Better that all of you leave right away."

Then Linji gave a shout and said: "People who lack the root of faith will never completely comprehend. You have been standing [here listening] a long time. Take care."

One day Linji came to [the city of] Henan-fu. The chief official there, a Mr. Wang, invited him to preach.

On this occasion [the Zen adept] Magu came forth [from the audience] and asked: "The bodhisattva of great compassion has a thousand hands and eyes—which is the correct eye?"

Linji said: "The bodhisattva of great compassion has a thousand hands and eyes—which is the correct eye? Speak quickly, speak quickly!"

Magu then dragged Linji down from the teacher's seat and took his place.

Linji went up to him and said: "I don't get it." Magu hesitated, trying to think, so Linji pulled him down off the seat and sat back down in it himself. Then Magu left [the teaching hall] and Linji got down from the teacher's seat.

Linji went up to the hall and said: "In this lump of red flesh, there's a true person without position always going in and out through your face. Those who have not experienced this, look, look!"

At the time there was a monk who came forth and asked: "What is the true person without position?"

Linji got down from the Zen bench, held the monk tight, and said: "Speak! Speak!"

The monk hesitated, trying to think of something to say. Linji pushed him away saying: "The true person without position—what a dry piece of shit!" Then he returned to the abbot's quarters.

Once when Linji went up to the hall, there was a monk who came forward and bowed. Linji then gave a shout. The monk said: "Old teacher, better not stick your nose into it." Linji said: "You tell me, where is it at?" The monk then shouted.

Another monk asked: "What is the true meaning of the Buddha Dharma?" Linji then gave a shout. The monk bowed. Linji said: "You tell me, was it a good shout or not?" The monk said: "The petty brigand has met complete defeat." Linji said: "Where was the fault?" The monk said: "A second offense is not allowed," and shouted.

One day when the head monks of the two halls met, they both shouted at the same time. A monk asked Linji: "Are there host and guest in this or not?" Linji said: "Host and guest are obvious."

[Later] Linji said: "If all of you want to understand Linji's phrase on guest and host, ask the two head monks." Then he left the teacher's seat.

Linji went up to the teaching hall. A monk asked: "What is the main meaning of the Buddha Dharma?" Linji held up the whisk. Then the monk shouted, and Linji hit him.

Another monk asked about the main meaning of the Buddha Dharma. As before, Linji held up the whisk. The monk shouted, and so did Linji. The monk hesitated, so Linji hit him.

Then Linji said to the assembly: "Everyone, for the sake of the Dharma, we do not shrink from losing our bodies and our lives. When I was at my late teacher Huangbo's place, three times I asked [to be told] the true meaning of the Buddha Dharma, and three times I got a beating bestowed on me. It was like being rubbed with a bitter herb. Right now I still think I deserve a beating. Who can give it to me?"

497a A monk came forward from the assembly and said; "I can give it to you." Linji picked up the staff and handed it to him. The monk hesitated to take it, so Linji hit him.

Linji went up to the teaching hall. A monk asked: "What is this business of walking on a sword edge?"

Linji said: "A disaster."

As the monk tried to think of something to say, Linji hit him.

Someone asked: "What about the Stone Room Workman? As he worked the treadmill, he forgot his feet were moving. Where did he go?" Linji said: "He was sunk deep in the source."

Then Linji said: "As long as there are people coming [to learn], I do not spurn them. I always take cognizance of where they are coming from. If they come like this [to ask me questions], it seems that they lose. If they do not come this way, they bind themselves without ropes. Never try to figure things out in a confused random way. Both understanding and not understanding are wrong. I say this quite plainly—I'll let everyone in the world condemn me. You have been standing a long time. Take care!"

Linji went up to the hall and said: "One person is up on the summit of a solitary peak with no way to come forth. One person is at the crossroads and neither faces nor turns away from [the passing scene]. Which is in front, which is behind? It's not Vimalakīrti or Mahāsattva Fu. Take care."

Linji went up to the hall and said: "There is one person who has been on the road through the ages without ever leaving home. There is one person who has left home but is not on the road. Which one ought to receive the offerings of humans and devas?"

Then he left the teacher's seat.

In the teaching hall a monk asked: "What is the first phrase?"

Linji said: "When the seal of the three essentials is lifted, the mark is narrow. There's no room to try to figure out the roles of the host and guest."

"What is the second phrase?"

Linji said: "How could wondrous subtle understanding have room for detached questions? How could skillful means spurn those with the potential to cut off the flow?"

"What is the third phrase?"

Linji said: "Look at the puppet theater—the one who pulls the strings is the person inside."

Linji further said: "Each phrase must have three mystic gates. Each mystic gate must have three essentials. There are provisional measures and there is functioning. How will all of you understand these things?"

Then Linji left the teacher's seat.

At a nighttime meeting Linji told the assembly: "Sometimes we take away the person but not the scene. Sometimes we take away the scene but not the person. Sometimes we take away both the person and the scene. Sometimes we don't take away the person or the scene."

At the time there was a monk who asked: "What is taking away the person but not the scene?"

Linji said: "The warm sun comes out, covering the earth with glittering brocade. The infant's hair hangs down as white as silk."

"What is taking away the scene but not the person?"

Linji said: "The royal command has already been put into practice all over the world. There are no more upheavals for the generals outside the border defenses."

"What is taking away both the person and the scene?"

Linji said: "There's no news from the rebel zones: they hold their areas on their own."

"What is not taking away either the person or the scene?"

Linji said: "The king ascends into the jewel palace and the old peasants sing for joy."

Then Linji said: "Those who study the Buddha Dharma these 497b
days must seek correct understanding. If you get it, birth and death will not stain you and it's up to you whether you go or stay. Don't seek [mystical states of] special excellence: these will come of themselves.

"O people of the Path, all the virtuous ones since antiquity have had a road to go beyond the ordinary human condition. When I instruct you, I just require that you do not accept other people's delusions. If you must act, then act, without any further laggard doubts.

"If students today do not succeed, where is their shortcoming? Their defect is that they do not believe in themselves. If you are unable to believe in yourself [as a vessel of the universal enlightened reality], you go off frantically following various objects, and get turned around by them, so that you have no independence. If you can put to rest the mind that is frantically seeking moment after moment, then you are no different from the buddhas and patriarchs.

"Do you want to get to know the buddhas and patriarchs? The one right here listening to the Dharma is they. It is because students cannot believe this that they go off frantically seeking outside. All you gain from seeking are just verbal marks of excellence—you will never find the living meaning of the enlightened teachers.

"Make no mistake about it, you Zen worthies. If you do not encounter this moment [of independent enlightenment], you will revolve in the triple world for thousands of eons, moving along following objects you think are good, being born in the bellies of donkeys and oxen.

"You people, in my view you are no different from Śākyamuni Buddha. In your manifold activities right now, what is lacking? Even amidst sensory life, the spiritual light never ceases. If you are able to see like this, you will be an unconcerned person your whole life long.

"O Virtuous Ones, there is no safe resting place in the triple world—it is like a house on fire. This is not where you will stay forever. The killing demon of impermanence [comes upon you] in an instant, without regard for rank or age.

"If you want to be no different from the buddhas and patriarchs, just don't seek outside yourself. A moment of your mind's pure light is the Dharmakāya Buddha inside your own house. A moment of your mind's light without discrimination is the

Sambhogakāya Buddha inside your own house. A moment of your mind's light with no distinctions is the Nirmāṇakāya Buddha within your own house. These three buddha-bodies are the person here before you now listening to the Dharma. They have their functional abilities just because they do not seek externally.

"Those who expound the sutras and śāstras take the three buddha-bodies as the ultimate paradigm. According to my view, it is not so. These three kinds of bodies are just names. They are also three dependencies. An ancient said: 'The bodies are established based on the meanings. The buddha-lands are assigned according to the embodiments.' You must realize clearly that [the concepts of] the body of reality and the land of reality-nature are just reflections of the light.

"All of you worthy people must get to know the person playing with the reflections of the light. This is the root source of all the buddhas, the place where all in the streams of the Path return home, wherever they are. This physical body of yours composed of the four elements does not know how to explain or listen to the Dharma. Your spleen and stomach and liver and gall bladder do not know how to explain or listen to the Dharma. What is it that can explain and listen to the Dharma? It's the one so clear and distinct right before your eyes, the formless solitary light. This is the one that knows how to preach and listen to the Dharma.

"If you can see like this, then you are no different from the 497c
buddhas and patriarchs. Just don't ever let [this perception of the light] be interrupted any more. Then, all that meets the eye is it. Because sentiments arise and [erroneous] knowledge blocks it off, the mentality shifts and you deviate away from essential being. This is why you revolve through the triple world subject to all kinds of suffering. But if you go by what I see, nothing is not most profound, nothing is not liberation.

"You people, the reality of mind is formless, and permeates all directions. In the eye it is called seeing, in the ear, hearing, in the nose, sense of smell. In the mouth it talks and argues, in the hands it holds and grasps, in the feet it moves and runs. Fundamentally it is a single pure light. It divides to form the six compounds [of sensory experience].

"If the [conditioned] mind is not there, everywhere is liberation. When I talk this way, where does the meaning lie? Because you people cannot stop your seeking minds, you fall into traps with the very empty and free teaching devices and perspectives of the ancients. If you adopt my view, you cut off the heads of the Sambhogakāya and Nirmāṇakāya Buddhas. You see the fulfillment of the [bodhisattvas'] ten stages as being like a guest pretending to be the son, and basic and wondrously activated enlightenment as fetters and chains. Arhats and pratyekas are like outhouse filth, bodhi and nirvana are pegs to tether donkeys to.

"Why are you like this? Just because you 'People of the Path' have not comprehended that the three measureless eons are empty and have not reached this emptiness. That is why you have these barriers and obstructions. If you were true People of the Path you would never be like this.

"You must be able to dissolve old karma according to circumstances, trusting to the movement of things and garbing yourself accordingly. When you need to walk, you walk; when you need to sit, you sit. There's never a thought of hoping for or seeking the fruits of buddhahood. Why must it be like this? An ancient said: 'If you want to seek buddhahood by creating karma, then [for you the concept] buddha is the harbinger of birth and death.'

"Worthy people, we must value the time. [You are wasting your chance] if you just intend to 'study Zen' and 'study the Path' as superficial adherents running busily back and forth, getting to recognize terms and phrases, seeking 'buddhas,' seeking 'patriarchs,' seeking 'enlightened teachers' [as you conceive of them]. You only have one father and mother: what else are you seeking? You should reflect back on yourself and see them.

"An ancient said: 'Yajñadatta [looked for his reflection in the wrong side of a mirror, and not seeing it, thought he had] lost his head. He only calmed down when he [realized his error] and stopped looking for his head.' Good people, what's essential is that in your everyday life you do not merely try to imitate models and patterns.

"There's one type of bald headed slaves [imitation monks] who do not recognize good and evil. [When they hear such talk] they immediately see spirits and ghosts, point to the east as the west, and entertain contradictory desires. This type we must spurn. Someday in front of Yama [the king of the underworld, who judges the dead,] they will have to swallow a red-hot iron ball. Men and women of good families are captured by this sort of wild fox spirit. They concoct strange things and blind many people. Someday they will be asked to pay for the food [they earned by deluding people].

"People, you must find true understanding. As you traverse the world, do not be deluded or confused by such malevolent sprites."

Linji taught the assembly saying: "The noble person is the one who has no concerns. Simply do not create any doings. Just be ordinary. If you seek outside and ask someone else to find your hands and feet for you, you've made a mistake.

"You just intend to seek Buddha. But 'Buddha' is a name, a 498a
word. Do you know the one that is seeking? All the buddhas and ancestral teachers in all lands in all times came forth just to seek the Dharma too. You people studying the Path now are also doing so in order to seek the Dharma. Only when you find the Dharma will you be finished. Before you find it, you will continue as before to revolve in the various planes of existence.

"What is the Dharma? The Dharma is the reality of mind. The reality of mind is formless. It pervades the ten directions. It is functioning here before our eyes. People cannot believe in it, so they accept names and words and seek intellectual ideas of the Buddha Dharma from written texts. They are as far off as can be.

"You people, when I preach the Dharma, what Dharma do I preach? I preach the Dharma of the mind-ground, so I can enter both ordinary and holy, both pure and defiled, both the real and the conventional. It's not that you are real or conventional, ordinary or holy, but that you can apply these names to everything, whereas the things [you call] real and conventional and ordinary and holy cannot apply these names to you. To take charge and act, without applying names any more—this is called the gist of the mystic message.

"I explain the Dharma differently from anyone else. If Mañjuśrī or Samantabhadra appear before me in some manifestation to ask about the Dharma, as soon as they open their mouths to ask for instruction, I've already sized them up. I am securely seated: when you people come to meet with me, I have already sized you all up. Why is it this way? Because my perception is different. Externally I do not seize upon ordinary or holy, and inwardly I do not abide in the basis. When you see all the way through things, there are no more doubts or deceptions."

Linji taught the assembly saying: "The Buddha Dharma is effortless: just be without concerns in your ordinary life, as you shit and piss and wear clothes and eat food. When tired, then lie down. Fools will laugh at you, but the wise will know. An ancient said: 'Those who make external efforts are all stupid and obstinate. Just act the master wherever you are, and where you stand is real.' When objects appear they cannot turn you around. Though the uninterrupted hellish karma of the habit energy of your past is still there, it spontaneously becomes the great ocean of liberation.

"These days students in general do not know the Dharma. They are like goats: whatever they encounter, they put in their mouths. They do not distinguish between the slaves and the free, the guests and the host. This type 'enter the Path' with twisted minds. Even though they cannot enter places where it's noisy, they call themselves true leavers of home. Actually they are true conventional worldlings.

"As for leavers of home, they must be able to perceive with true understanding in ordinary life. They distinguish enlightenment and delusion, true and false, ordinary and holy. If you can make these distinctions, you are called a true leaver of home. If you cannot tell deluding from enlightening influences, then you have left one home [ordinary life] only to enter another home [cultish 'religious' allegiances]. Then you are called a sentient being creating karma, not a true leaver of home.

"Right now there's something where enlightenment and delusion share the same substance undivided. It's like water and milk mixed together: the king goose drinks only the milk. People of the Path with clear eyes will reject both delusion and enlightenment. If you love holy things and hate ordinary things, you float and sink in 498b
the sea of birth and death."

Someone asked: "What are enlightenment and delusion?"

Linji said: "A moment when your mind is in doubt is delusion. If you can comprehend that the myriad phenomena are unborn, that [deluded] mind is like an illusory transformation, so that you are everywhere pure, this is enlightenment. So enlightenment and delusion are the two objects, defilement and purity.

"In my view, there are no buddhas and no sentient beings, no ancient and no modern. Those who attain, attain without cultivation, without realization, without gain, and without loss: for them there is never anything else but reality. 'Even if there is anything that goes beyond this, I would say that it is like a dream or a magical illusion.' This is what I am saying.

"You people, the solitary light right here before our eyes right now listening clearly to the Dharma—this one does not get stuck anywhere—it extends throughout the ten directions, independent of the triple world. It enters all circumstances, but they cannot turn it around: in every moment it extends through the realm of reality.

"When you meet buddhas, you speak to buddhas; when you meet ancestral teachers, you talk to ancestral teachers; when you meet arhats, you talk to arhats; when you meet hungry ghosts, you talk to hungry ghosts. Everywhere you go in your travels through the various lands you teach and transform sentient beings without ever departing from this one moment of mindfulness. Wherever you are the pure light extends in all directions and the myriad phenomena are one suchness.

"You people, only Today [the day of enlightenment] do you know that fundamentally there are no concerns. Because you cannot fully believe this, every moment you are frantically seeking. You throw away a head and pick up a head, unable to stop yourself.

"The bodhisattvas of round and sudden enlightenment enter the realm of reality to manifest their bodies, abiding in the pure land, spurning ordinary life and rejoicing in the sagely. For them grasping and rejecting are not yet forgotten, and ideas of defiled and pure still remain. In the view of the Zen school, it is not this way. It's simply that there is no other time but right now.

"What I say is all medicine to treat the diseases of this one period. There is no real doctrine here. If you can see things like this, you are a real leaver of home, worth ten thousand ounces of gold a day.

"Don't be in a hurry to get the teacher's seal of approval across your forehead so that you can claim to understand Zen and understand the Path. Even if your eloquence is like a waterfall, all of this only creates more hellish karma. If you are a person who is genuinely studying the Path, you don't look for worldly faults. What you must seek is correct understanding. You are done only when you arrive at real correct perception that is completely illuminated."

Someone asked: "What is real correct perception?"

Linji said: "It means that wherever you enter, whether it be ordinary or holy, defiled or pure, whether it be any of the buddhalands, or Maitreya's tower, or the realm of Vairocana, in all places where lands appear being formed, abiding, decaying, or empty, in all places where buddhas appear in the world, turn the wheel of the Dharma, and enter back into nirvana—in all these places, real correct perception means that you see no signs of coming and going, that birth and death cannot be found. Then you enter the
498c unborn realm of reality, wandering through all lands. You enter the world hidden in the lotus, where you see the emptiness of all things, none of which are real.

"The mother of all the buddhas is just the independent person of the Path [within you] who hears the Dharma. Thus, enlightenment is born from having no dependencies. If you can awaken without dependencies, enlightenment too is without attainment. If you can manage to see like this, this is real correct perception.

"Students do not understand because they cling to names and sayings. They are obstructed by the names 'ordinary' and 'holy.' Thus they block their eye for the Path and do not find clear understanding. The scriptural teachings are all openly revealed explanations, but students do not understand them. Instead, they go to the words and phrases to produce interpretations. All of this is being dependent and falling into cause and effect, so birth and death in the triple world are inevitable.

"If you want to get the freedom to go or stay, to take off or put on birth and death, then right now try to recognize the person who is listening to the Dharma.

"This person has no form, no marks, no basis, no root, nowhere it abides, but it is leaping with life. In all its many kinds of activities, it functions without location. Therefore, if you search for it, the farther away it is, and if you seek it, the more you go against it. It is called the esoteric secret.

"People, do not accept this imaginary companion: later it will revert to impermanence. In this world, what are you looking for as liberation? You are looking for a mouthful of food to eat, some simple clothes to wear, a way to pass the time. You must pay a visit to an enlightened teacher. Don't just follow your routines and pursue pleasure. Time should be valued. Everything is impermanent from moment to moment. On a crude level we are harried by earth, water, fire, and air; on a subtle level we are pressed by the four aspects, birth, abiding, variation, and demise. Right now you people should get to know the four formless realms, so you can avoid being knocked back and forth by circumstances."

Someone asked: "What are the four formless realms?"

Linji said: "When you have a moment of doubt in your mind, you are obstructed by earth. When you have a moment of love in your mind, you are drowned in water. When you have a moment of anger in your mind, you are burned by fire. When you have a moment of joy in your mind, you are blown around by air.

"If you can perceive this, then you will not be turned around by objects and circumstances, but rather, wherever you are, you will use them. Then you can appear in the east and disappear in the west, or appear in the south and disappear in the north; you can appear in the middle and disappear around the edge or appear around the edge and disappear in the middle. You walk on water as if it were earth and on earth as if it were water. Why are you like this [at this stage]? Because you have comprehended that the four elements [earth, water, fire, air] are like dreams or magical illusions.

"People, the one in your listening to the Dharma right now is not the four elements that comprise you. Rather, it can employ the four elements in you. If you can see like this, then you are free to go or stay.

"In my view, there are no things to despise and avoid. If you love what's holy, [I remind you:] 'holy' is just a name. There are some students who go to Mt. Wutai to look for Mañjuśrī [there in his legendary abode]. Already they are in error: there is no Mañjuśrī on Mt. Wutai. Do you want to know Mañjuśrī? This functioning here right before your eyes has never been any different [from Mañjuśrī]. To have no doubts anywhere—this is the living Mañjuśrī. In the moment of nondifferentiating light in your mind,
499a the real Samanta-bhadra is everywhere. When in a moment of
mind you can free yourself from bondage, and be liberated wherever you are, this is Avalokiteśvara. In the teaching of samādhi, [these three bodhisattvas] take turns as central figure and companions. When they come forth, it is for a certain period. Each one is all three and all three of them are one. Only when you understand like this can you read the scriptures properly."

Linji taught the assembly saying: "You people who study the Path now must have faith in yourselves [as endowed with buddha-nature]. You must not seek externally. You always fall into traps with the free and easy devices and perspectives [used in teaching by the enlightened ones] and cannot tell crooked from straight. As for buddhas and patriarchs, these are things in the scriptural teachings. When someone brings up a saying, whether it comes from the hidden or the manifest part of the teachings, you immediately have doubts and look everywhere asking other people [what the saying means]. You are really confused. Really great people do not carry on in this way, discussing rulers and rebels, right and wrong, beauty and wealth, and passing their days in idle talk.

"Here I don't care if you are monk or lay. Whenever people come [to learn], I know all about them. No matter where you come from, if all you have is names and phrases [to repeat], it's all a dream-like illusion.

"If I see someone who is able to ride on objects and circumstances, this is the mystic essence of all the buddhas. The realm of buddhahood does not announce itself as the realm of buddhahood. Rather, [buddhahood] is when an independent person of the Path comes forth riding on objects and circumstances.

"[If I am such an independent person of the Path], when someone comes forth and asks me about seeking buddha, I come forth in response to the realm of purity. If someone asks me about being a bodhisattva, I come forth in response to the realm of compassion. If someone asks me about enlightenment, I come forth in response to the realm of wondrous purity. If someone asks me about nirvana, I come forth in response to the realm of silent stillness. Though there are myriad kinds of realms, the person [who responds to them] is no different. Thus does [the enlightened person] manifest form in response to beings, like the moon reflected in the water.

"All of you, if you wish to be in accord with the Dharma, you must be such a really great person. If you are dependent and weak, you will not succeed. Ordinary crockery is not good enough to store the pure elixir in. Those who are great vessels are not subject to people's delusions. Wherever they are, they act the master—their standpoint is always the real.

"Though [such delusions] may come, you must not accept any of them. If you have a moment of doubt, delusion enters your mind. 'When a bodhisattva doubts, the delusive demon of birth and death has its way.' Just manage to put a stop to your thoughts, and do not do any more external seeking. When things come, shine through them. You must be certain that in that which is functioning here and now, there is not a single thing to be concerned about. In a moment of mind you give birth to the triple world, follow its entangling causes, and are covered over by its objects and circumstances, dividing them into six realms of sensory experience.

"As you function responsively right now, is anything lacking? In a single instant, you enter both pure and defiled; you enter Maitreya's tower; you enter the lands of the eye of reality, the eye of knowledge, and the eye of wisdom. Everywhere you wander, you see only empty names [not real entities]."

Someone asked: "What are the lands of the three eyes?"

Linji said: "Together you and I enter the land of purity and subtle wonder. We put on robes of purity and talk of the Dharmakāya
499b Buddha. We also enter the land without differentiations, where we put on robes of nondifferentiation and talk of the Sambhogakāya Buddha. We also enter the land of liberation, where we put on robes of light and talk of the Nirmāṇakāya Buddha. These three lands are all dependent on transformation.

"Those who specialize in the sutras and śāstras take the Dharmakāya as the basis, and the Sambhogakāya and Nirmāṇakāya as the functioning. The way I see it, the Dharmakāya cannot preach the Dharma. Thus the ancient [Huayan adept Kuiji, also known as] Cien said: 'The bodies are established based on the meanings and the lands assigned according to their embodiments.' For the Dharmakāya, the body of reality, there is the land of reality-nature. We must realize clearly that these are constructs. The lands of the spiritual powers based on this reality are nothing but an empty fist [pretending to hold a treasure] or a handful of yellow leaves [passed off as gold] used to deceive small children [and lure them out of the burning house of worldly life]. What juice are you looking for from [such] brambles and thorns and dry bones?

"Outside of mind there is nothing, and what is within mind is also unattainable. What are you looking for? All of you people everywhere talk of having cultivation and having realization, but don't make this mistake. Even if you gain something from cultivation, it is just the karma of birth and death. You say you cultivate the six perfections and the myriad practices, but as I see it you are just building karma. When you seek Buddha and seek the Dharma, you are creating hellish karma. When you seek to be bodhisattvas, you are also creating karma. When you read the sutras, you are also creating karma. The buddhas and ancestral teachers were people without concerns. Thus they make nothing but pure karma, whether they are in the defiled realm of contrived action, or in the stainless realm without contrived action.

"There are a certain kind of blind shave-pates who eat their fill of food and then go to sit in meditation. They grab hold of wayward thoughts and do not let them go on. Weary of noise, they seek quietude. These are not Buddhist methods. The ancestral teacher [Shenhui of Heze] said: 'If you fixate your mind and contemplate stillness, hold up your mind for outer awareness and hold in your mind for inner realization, freeze your mind and enter stable concentration, this is all contrived activity.'

"It is the person in you who is listening to the Dharma this way right now. How can you try to cultivate this person or realize him or adorn him? He is not something that can be cultivated or adorned. If we would have him adorned, in fact all things are what adorn him.

"You people must not mistake what I say. [You will go wrong] if you seize upon the words in this old teacher's mouth and think they are the real Path, if you think you as people of ordinary mentality cannot presume to try to fathom or assess the inconceivable lessons of an enlightened teacher and experienced adept. As soon as you adopt this opinion, you have turned your back on this eye of enlightenment [within us all]. Then you are shivering cold and speechless like a baby donkey on a hill of ice.

"I am not presuming to slander the enlightened teachers, lest I create mouth-karma. Dear people, only the great enlightened teachers can presume to knock down the buddhas and patriarchs, judge the rights and wrongs of the world, repudiate and set aside the scriptural teachings, and rebuke and insult all you little ones. They look for people amidst favorable and adverse currents.

"I have looked for a fixed karmic identity constantly, but even the smallest particle of one cannot be found. Like nervous new brides, would-be Zen people are afraid to be driven out of their homes, afraid that they will not be given food to eat, that they will be uneasy and unhappy. Ever since ancient times, the former generations of enlightened people have been met everywhere by disbelief. Only after they had been driven out did people begin to realize how precious they were. But if people everywhere all were willing to accept them, what good would that do? This is why [we
499c say], with one roar of the lion, the fox's brain bursts.

"Everywhere there are those who say that there is a Path that can be cultivated and a truth that can be realized. You tell me, what path, what truth? What is lacking in your present functioning? Where will you cultivate and repair it? The younger generation of would-be Zen people do not understand this, so they believe in these wild fox spirits. When they explain things, they tie people down. They say that enlightenment can be attained only when truth and conduct are in accord and you guard yourself from misdeeds of thought, speech, and action. This kind of talk is like springtime drizzle.

"A man of old [Sikong Benjing, a disciple of the Sixth Patriarch] said: 'When on the road you meet a person who has consummated the Path, above all do not face toward the Path.' Thus it is said that if a person cultivates the Path [in a contrived dualistic manner] but does not travel the Path [as all-encompassing nondualistic reality], then myriad kinds of false scenes and distorted perspectives soon arise all around. When the sword of wisdom comes out, there's not a single thing—the bright side doesn't show but the dark side is illuminated.

"Therefore, the ancients said, 'Ordinary mind is the Path.' Worthy people, what are you looking for? The independent person of the Path who is here before your eyes right now listening to the

Dharma is clearly obvious. It has never been lacking. If you want to be no different from the buddhas and patriarchs, just see like this. Don't plunge into doubts and errors. If you go from mind-moment to mind-moment without deviating [from this perception], you are called a buddha. If your mind deviates, then reality-nature and form separate; if your mind does not deviate, then reality-nature and form are no different."

Someone asked: "What does it mean to go from mind-moment to mind-moment without deviating?"

Linji said: "If you try to ask, you have already deviated, and reality-nature and form have been separated. Make no mistake about it, people. All phenomena worldly and world-transcending are without a real fixed identity of their own, they have no inherent nature. There are just empty names, and names are empty too. If you go on this way accepting these empty names as real things, you are making a great mistake. Even if they are there, they are all objects and scenes dependent on transformation [for their temporary being]. There is also such a thing as depending on bodhi and nirvana and liberation, depending on the three bodies of buddha, depending on objective wisdom, depending on bodhisattvas and buddhas. What are you looking for in lands dependent upon transformation? Even the multi-part scriptural teachings of the three vehicles are just old paper for wiping away dirt. Buddha is an illusion, an apparition. The ancestral teachers were just old monks.

"Weren't you born from your mama? If you seek buddha, you are controlled by the delusion 'buddha.' If you seek the ancestral teachers, you are bound by the delusion 'ancestral teachers.' As long as you have seeking, it's all suffering. Better to have no concerns at all.

"There's a kind of bald monk who says to students: 'Buddha is the ultimate. You only achieve enlightenment after the fulfillment of the results of three immeasurable eons of cultivating practice.' Good people, if you think Buddha is the ultimate, then why did he lie down and die at the age of eighty between the twin trees in the grove at Kuśinagara? Where is Buddha today? It's clear that

he was born and died no different from us. You might say that the thirty-two auspicious marks and the eighty excellent qualities make him a buddha, and a wheel-turning sage king must be a tathāgata. But you should understand clearly that these are all illusory apparitions. The man of old [Mahāsattva Fu] said: 'The tathāgatas take on bodily form in order to accord with worldly
500a feelings. Fearing people would form nihilistic views, he provisionally established some empty names, temporarily talking of the thirty-two marks and the eighty excellent qualities. These too are empty words. If there is a body, it's not the essential body of enlightenment. Formlessness is the true shape.'

"You may say that Buddha has six spiritual powers that are inconceivable. But all the devas, the immortals, the asuras, and the powerful demons also have spiritual powers. Does this mean they must be buddhas too? Don't go wrong about this. The asuras did battle with Indra, king of the gods, and when they were defeated, they gathered together their host of 84,000 and hid in a hole in a lotus fiber. Isn't this supernatural? All these examples I've cited are cases of spiritual powers due to karma and dependent [on contrived techniques]. In the case of the Buddha's six spiritual powers, it is not so. Buddha enters form, sound, smell, taste, touch, and concepts without being deluded by them. Thus, since he has arrived at the emptiness of form, sound, smell, taste, touch, and concepts, these cannot bind the independent person of the Path. For him, even the defiled body of form, sensation, conception, motivation, and consciousness is in itself a spiritual power for walking upon the earth.

"Good people, the real Buddha is formless; the real Dharma has no marks. The way you are acting is to erect models and patterns based upon the illusory transformations [which were provisionally put forward in the Buddhist teachings]. Even if you get something from this, you are all wild fox spirits. This is not real Buddhism at all, but the view of outsiders.

"People who study the Path genuinely do not grasp buddhas or bodhisattvas or arhats; they do not grasp attainments of special excellence within the triple world. They are transcendent and free and on their own—they are not constrained by things. Even if heaven and earth turn upside down, they are not in doubt. If all the buddhas of the ten directions appear before them, they feel no joy. If [all the torments of] the hungry ghosts, the animals, and the beings in hell appear before them, they feel no fear. Why are they like this? They see the emptiness of all phenomena, which exist through transformation and don't exist without it. They see that the triple world is only mind, and the myriad things are only consciousness. Therefore, why bother to grasp [what are really] dreamlike illusions and apparitions?

"There is only the person in all of you right here and now listening to the Dharma. This person enters fire without being burned and water without being drowned. This person enters the mires of hell as if strolling in a garden sightseeing. This person enters the planes of the hungry ghosts and animals without being subject to their suffering. Why so? Because for this person there is nothing to reject, nothing to avoid.

"If you love the holy and hate the ordinary, you float and sink in the sea of birth and death. Affliction exists because of mind: if you have no mind, how can affliction hold you? If you do not try to discriminate and grasp forms, naturally you find the Path that instant.

"If you try to learn as a shallow adherent running busily here and there, then through three immeasurable eons you will always return in the end to birth and death. Far better to go into the Zen forest without concerns, fold up your legs on a meditation bench, and sit.

"All over the country there are students who come [to teachers with the wrong attitude]. As soon as host and guest meet, these students bring out a phrase to test the teacher they are facing. These students bring up some teaching device or provisional formulation and throw it down as a challenge to the teacher to see if he knows it or not. If the teacher recognizes the scene, these students hold fast and throw him into a pit. If the students are the ordinary type, after this they seek for a saying from the teacher, which they appropriate as before [to take elsewhere to 'test' other teachers], and exclaim how wise the teacher is. I say to such students: 'You know nothing of good and bad!'

500b "An enlightened teacher takes a teaching perspective and confronts the student with it. If the student can tell what's going on, and act the master at every move, and is not confused by the teaching scene, then the enlightened teacher shows half a body, and the student gives a shout. The teacher then enters upon the road of differentiating phrases to try to knock the student over. If the student then calls the teacher a bald old slave who does not know good from bad, the teacher exclaims happily that this is a genuine person of the Path.

"Everywhere there are [supposed] teachers who cannot tell wrong from right. When students come to ask them about bodhi and nirvana and the wisdoms of the three bodies of buddha, these blind teachers immediately give them explanations. If they are rebuked by the students, they give them a beating and say they have no sense of etiquette. But since these [supposed] teachers have no eyes, they should not get mad at other people.

"There are phony monks who do not know good from bad, who point to the east and call it the west, who entertain contradictory desires and love inscrutable sayings. Look and see if they do not bear the telltale marks of false teachers. They know some enlightenment stories [but not when to use them]. When students do not understand [such random 'instructions'], the pretended teachers soon lose their tempers. This type are all wild fox spirits and hideous monsters. They are laughed at by good students, who say to them: 'Blind old bald-pate slaves, you are confusing everyone in the world.'

"You people of the Path, those who leave home must learn the Path. Take me for example. In the past I was concerned with the vinaya, and I also researched the sutras and śāstras. Only later did I realize that these are medicines to cure the world, openly revealed explanations. But then I put them aside for a time and went travelling to study Zen. Later I met a great enlightened teacher [Huangbo] and only then did the eye of the Path become clear for me. I began to understand the world's teachers, and to know who was misguided and who was correct. If you do not understand immediately when your mama gives birth to you, then you need direct experiential research, refining and polishing, until one morning there's spontaneous insight.

"Good people, if you want to get your views and perceptions in accord with the Dharma, just do not accept people's delusions. Wherever you meet them, inside or outside, immediately slay them. [Even cherished concepts like] buddha, patriarch, arhat, parents, relatives, and household—as soon as you meet them, slay them. Only then will you find liberation. Unconstrained by things, you penetrate through to sovereign independence.

"Throughout the country, most who study the Path try to depend on things to do so. I start hitting from there. If they use their hands, I hit them on the hands. If they use their mouths, I hit them in the mouth. If they use their eyes, I hit them in the eye. Almost none of them come forth independently and freely. Most have fallen into the traps around the free and easy teaching devices and perspectives of the people of old.

"There is no fixed doctrine to give to people, only methods to cure diseases and release bonds. You people of the Path, who come from all over the country, should try to come forth without depending on anything. I want to talk things over with you. For 500c
years on end there has been no one [independent, capable of understanding Buddhism, to communicate with]. [Those who have come] have all been wild fox spirits and ghosts haunting the forests and fields, who gnaw at random on all the lumps of shit. These blind [false seekers] wrongly consume the faithful offerings of many people, proclaiming themselves to be leavers of home, but they adopt this kind of [dependent wild fox spirit] view.

"I tell you, there is no Buddha, no Dharma, no cultivation, no realization. What are you trying to find this way as a shallow adherent? Blind people [who reify these concepts] are placing a head upon a head [imposing objects of seeking upon spontaneous reality].

"What are you lacking? Good people, what's functioning right now before your eyes is no different from the buddhas and patriarchs. Because you do not believe this, you go outside to seek. Make no mistake about it: there are no external phenomena, and the internal too is unattainable. Rather than seize upon my words, you had better stop and rest and be without concerns. What has already arisen, do not continue. What has not yet arisen, do not let arise. This is better than ten years of wandering.

"There are not so many kinds in my view. It is just a matter of being ordinary, of wearing clothes and eating food and passing the time without concerns. You come from all over, and you all have [false states of] mind. You seek the Buddha and you seek the Dharma. You seek liberation, you seek to leave the triple world. You fools, where do you want to go when you leave the triple world?

"'Buddha' and 'patriarch' are just honorific names. Do you want to know the triple world? It is not apart from the mind-ground in you listening to the Dharma right now. A mental moment of craving is the world of desire. A mental moment of anger is the world of form. A mental moment of ignorance is the formless world. These are all furnishings inside your own house. The triple world does not announce, 'I am the triple world.' Rather, it is you who give it this name, you, the person here right now, luminous and aware, shining on the myriad things, judging and assessing the world.

"Good people, the physical body composed of the four great elements is impermanent. [All the parts of your body], your spleen and stomach and liver and hair and nails and teeth, just reveal the emptiness of all things.

"Where your mind stops for a moment, this is called the bodhi tree, [the site of enlightenment]. Your mind being unable to stop is called the tree of ignorance. There is nowhere that ignorance abides; it has no beginning and no end. If from moment to moment your mind cannot stop [its deluded stream of consciousness], then you climb the tree of ignorance. Then you enter among the various kinds of beings in the six planes of existence to wear fur on your body and horns on your head. If you can manage to stop, this is the body and realm of purity. If you are unborn for a moment, then you climb the tree of enlightenment. Then the light spontaneously shines, the light of the deliberate transformation bodies created by spiritual powers in the triple world and the bodies of the bliss of the Dharma and the joy of Zen. You think of clothing and get a thousand bolts of the finest silk; you think of food and every flavor is provided to you. There are no more untoward sicknesses.

"Enlightenment abides nowhere. Therefore, there is no attaining it. What else is there for really great people to be in doubt about? Who is the one before your very eyes functioning? Take hold and act: don't affix names. This is the mystic message. If you can see things this way, there is nothing to despise or avoid. An ancient said: 'Mind revolves following the myriad objects. Where 501a
it revolves is surely obscure. If, following the flow, you can recognize its true nature, there is no joy or sorrow.'

"Good people, in the understanding of the Zen school, death and life follow in cycles. People trying to learn must examine this closely. When host and guest meet, there is talk back and forth.

"[The teacher, who should be the 'host', the representative of reality and channel of truth] sometimes manifests form in response to beings, sometimes functions with the whole essence, sometimes uses provisional devices to appear happy or angry, sometimes shows only half his body, sometimes rides a lion, sometimes rides an elephant king.

"If the student is genuine, he or she immediately shouts [as if to say to the teacher:] 'Already you have brought out a bowl of glue!' If the teacher does not know this perspective, then he falls within the other one's perspective as a rote imitator. The student then shouts [as if to say:] 'I will not let you go!' This is a mortal disease, beyond curing. It is called the guest observing the host [the genuine student seeing through the false teacher].

"Alternatively, the teacher might not bring out anything at all. [Instead] as the student asks about things, he takes them away. The teacher never relents as everything is taken away from the student. This is called the host observing the guest [genuine teacher and beginning student].

"Sometimes a student appears before a teacher in response to a pure realm [of mystic experience]. The teacher recognizes this realm, holds it fast, and hurls it into a pit. The student exclaims, 'What a great enlightened teacher!' The teacher says, 'Bah! You don't know good from bad.' The student then bows in homage. This is called host observing host [genuine teacher and accomplished student].

"Sometimes a student appears before a teacher bearing fetters and chains [of subjective views and ideas]. The teacher hangs another load of chains around his neck, and the student rejoices. Neither one can discern the other. This is called guest seeing guest [false teacher, false student].

"Worthy people, when I mention things this way, it is to pick out delusions and deviations [operating in the guise of Buddhism] so that you may know what is twisted and what is correct.

"People of the Path, actual sentiments are very difficult, and the Buddha Dharma is abstruse and dark. Even if you understand easily and quickly, I will refute your understandings for you all day long. Students never get to rest within their opinions. Thousands and thousands of times their feet plod through lands of total darkness, without a single form, where the solitary light is clear and distinct.

"Students do not have faith in themselves, so they go to words and phrases to generate interpretations. They reach the age of fifty as mere superficial adherents carrying corpses on their backs, bearing their burdens, running all around the world. Someday they will be pressed to pay back all the travel money [they have wasted in 'seeking' without finding].

"Worthy people, I say to you that there are no external phenomena. You as students do not understand, so you interpret this to mean that all things are internal. Then you sit leaning against a wall with your tongue pressed to the roof of your mouth, motionless in profound clarity. You seize upon this as the gate of the patriarchs, as the Buddha Dharma. How wrong you are! In fact, if you grasp this scene of motionless purity as right, you are accepting ignorance as your master. Referring to this, an ancient said: 'The deep dark pit of profound clarity is to be feared.'

"But if you accept movement as the one that's right, then since all the plants and trees move, they must be the Path. Movement is due to the element air; motionlessness to the element earth. Neither movement or motionlessness has any fixed identity of its own.
If you grasp it in movement, it is in motionlessness; if you grasp it 501b
in motionlessness, it is in movement. Like a fish swimming below the surface of a stream, it stirs up waves as it leaps around. Good people, movement and motionlessness are two perspectives. If you are an independent person of the Path, you use both.

"When students from all over come here, I judge them in terms of three kinds of basic capacity. When those of lower capacity come, I take away their objects but not their methods. When those of higher capacity come, I take away both their objects and their methods. When those of the highest capacity come, I take away neither the objects nor the methods nor the person. If people come with views that go beyond patterns, here I function with the whole essence, not grading basic capacity. At this point, the place where the student puts his or her energy is impervious to the wind [of deluding influences]. Like sparks struck from stone or a flash of lightning, it's gone by.

"Whether your eye is steady or moves, there's no contact. If you try to do something with mind, you go wrong; if thoughts stir, you go against it. For those who understand, it's right before their eyes, nowhere else.

"Worthy people, you run around as shallow adherents with your bowls and sacks and shitty burdens seeking the Buddha and seeking the Dharma. This one right now frantically seeking—do you know him? He's leaping with life—it's just that he has no root or stem. He cannot be hemmed in or knocked apart. He's farther away if you seek him. If you don't seek, he's right before your eyes, his spirit voice in your ear. If people do not believe this, they labor in vain for hundreds of years.

"You people of the Path, in an instant you enter the world hidden in the lotus, you enter the land of Vairocana, you enter the land of liberation, the land of penetrating spiritual powers, the land of purity, the realm of reality. You enter among both defiled and pure, both ordinary and holy, and even among the hungry ghosts and animals. You seek everywhere, but nowhere do birth and death appear, only empty names, illusory transformations, and flowers in the sky, not worth grasping. Gain and loss, affirmation and denial, are at once abandoned.

"You people of the Path, I received the Buddha Dharma truly, following Master Magu, Master Danxia, Master Mazu, Master Guizong, and Master Shizhu: on a single road, we travelled all over China. No one believed in them, and all were slandered. For example, Mazu's actions were pure and unmixed, but none of his three hundred or five hundred students saw his intent. Guizong, the master on [Mt.] Lushan, was independent and genuine, but students could not figure out the locus of his functioning: he [sometimes] went with and [sometimes] went against, so they all became flustered. Master Danxia appreciated the pearl [of wisdom] in both hidden and manifest forms, but when students came, they were all rebuked. Magu's functioning was bitter as a philodendron, and none could approach him. Shizhu's functioning was to seek people at the point of his arrow, so all who came to him were terrified.

"As for my functioning today, I create and destroy correctly, playing freely with spiritual transformations, entering all perspectives, unconcerned everywhere I go. Objects and scenes cannot turn me around.

"When someone comes seeking, I go out and look at him, but
501c he does not recognize me. I then put on various kinds of 'clothes'. Students give birth to interpretations, and always go for my words. How painful! Blind monks and people without eyes take the clothes I am wearing and recognize them as blue, yellow, red, white. I take them off and enter into the realm of purity. As soon as the students see this, they feel happiness and desire. When I take off [the garment of purity] too, students lose heart, and run off in

crazy confusion saying I have no clothes. I say to them: 'Do you recognize the person in me who is putting on the clothes?' Suddenly they turn their heads around and they recognize me.

"Good people, do not accept the 'clothes' [as the person]. The clothes cannot move: it's the person who puts them on. There is the garment of purity, the garment of birthlessness, the garment of bodhi, the garment of nirvana, the garments of the buddhas and patriarchs. Whatever has to do with words and names and phrases and texts is all a matter of changing 'clothes'. Words are formed by being brought forth from the ocean of vital energy at the navel and coming out through the teeth. Obviously they are all illusory transformations.

"Good people, you generate the karma of speech outwardly, and inwardly you show [dualistic perception of] mind and its objects. All the states of mind you have because of your thoughts are all 'clothes'. [Your problem] is that you accept the 'clothes' that the person puts on as something real. Even if you pass through countless eons of time, all you do is keep changing clothes, cycling through the triple world, revolving in birth and death. It is better to have no concerns, to meet without recognizing and talk together without knowing each other's names.

"When students these days do not succeed, it is generally because they accept words and terminology as [the route to] understanding. In big notebooks, they copy down the words of dead old men; they wrap them up in layers and layers of cloth, and don't let other people see them. They say that these are mystic messages, and guard them most seriously. This is a great error. I ask you blind ones with many births to go, what juice are you looking for on dry bones?

"Some do not know good from bad. They seize upon ideas from the scriptural teachings to discuss and compose commentaries with. This is like putting a lump of shit in your mouth, then spitting it out and giving it to someone else. It also resembles the way people in conventional life relay official orders along to each other. Thus do this type pass their whole lives in vain. They call themselves leavers of home, but if they are asked about the Buddha Dharma, they are tongue-tied and speechless, with eyes popping out and mouths pulled down in a frown. Even if Maitreya appeared in the world, this type would move to another world to suffer in hell.

"Good people, you hurry around everywhere, but what are you seeking? You have worn your soles flat. There is no Buddha that can be sought, no Path that can be achieved, no Dharma that can be attained. If you seek outside for a buddha with form, it is not like the real you. Do you want to know your fundamental mind? It's neither merged with nor apart from [birth and death, karmic consciousness]. The real Buddha is formless, the real Path has no body, the real Dharma has no marks. The three are fused together, joined in one place. But since you cannot discern this, you are just ordinary, busy, confused sentient beings [in the grips] of karmic consciousness."

Someone asked Linji: "What are the real Buddha, the real Dharma, and the real Path? Please instruct us."

Linji said: "Buddha is the mind's purity. Dharma is the mind's light. The Path is the pure light that is unobstructed everywhere.
502a The three are one. All three are empty names, not real. For genuine people of the Path, this mind is not interrupted from moment to moment.

"When the great teacher Bodhidharma came from India, he was just looking for people who do not accept other people's delusions. Later he met the Second Patriarch, who understood at a single word, and finally realized that up till then he had been making his efforts in vain.

"The way I see today is no different from the buddhas and patriarchs. If you get it at the first phrase, you are a teacher to buddhas and patriarchs. If you get it at the second phrase, you are a teacher of humans and devas. If you get it at the third phrase, you cannot even save yourself."

Someone asked: "What is the idea of the coming from the West?"

Linji said: "If you have intentional ideas, you cannot save yourself."

The questioner said: "Given there were no intentional ideas, how did the Second Patriarch find the Dharma?"

Linji said: "He found it without attainment."

"Given that he did not attain, what is the meaning of not attaining?"

Linji said: "Because your mind is frantically seeking everywhere and cannot stop, the Patriarch said to you: 'Fie on you, people, you are using a head to seek a head.' If under the impact of his words, you can turn the light around and reflect back, then you will not seek elsewhere any more. You realize that mind and body are no different from the buddhas and patriarchs. Only this direct and immediate freedom from concerns is called finding the Dharma."

[Linji continued:] "Worthy people, right now it is through lack of any alternative that I give verbal assessments and come out with so many unclean things. You should not mistake what I say. In my view, these many kinds of truths [I provisionally offer here] do not really exist. When I must use them, I use them; if not, I stop.

"Now in many areas, they talk of the six pāramitās and the myriad practices, and consider these to be the Buddha Dharma. I say that these are in the realm of adornment and the doings of enlightenment; they are not the Buddha Dharma itself. Even if you uphold a vegetarian diet and discipline as if your life depended on it, if the eye of the Path is not clear, you will have to discharge your debt—someday you will be pressed for repayment of the food money [that monks receive from the pious]. Why so? If you enter the Path without comprehending its inner truth, you will return to bodily form to pay back the offerings of the faithful.

"Some elders reach advanced age, but for them the tree [of enlightenment] does not grow. They may even live in solitude on a lone peak, eating once a day before dawn and sitting without ever lying down, practicing the Path day and night, but they are people creating karma. Some may even give away all they have, royal cities and wives and children and splendid surroundings, and even their very bodies, their heads, their eyes, their marrow, their brains. But all such views are causes of suffering for body and mind, which will bring on pain as the result.

"It's better to be without concerns, pure and at one. Then even if the bodhisattvas who have fulfilled the ten stages look for your tracks, they can never be found. Then all the heavens will rejoice, the earth spirits will hold up your feet, and all the buddhas of the ten directions will acclaim you. Why is it like this? Because [then] the person of the Path [within you] who is listening to the Dharma right now will be functioning without traces."

Someone asked: "The buddha [called] Great Pervasive Excellent Wisdom sat on the site of enlightenment for ten eons, but the Buddha Dharma, reality of enlightenment, did not appear before him, and he did not fulfill the Buddhist Path. What does this mean?"

502b Linji said: "[The name] 'Great Pervasive' means that you yourself in all places are arriving at and comprehending the fact that the myriad phenomena have no fixed identity and no absolute characteristics. 'Excellent Wisdom' means you have no doubts anywhere and do not grasp anything. 'Buddha' means the pure light of the mind penetrating through the realm of reality—this is named 'Buddha.' The ten eons sitting on the site of enlightenment refers to the ten pāramitās. 'The Buddha Dharma did not appear before him' in that Buddha is fundamentally unborn, and the Dharma is fundamentally indestructible, so how would [Buddha Dharma, the reality of the enlightened ones] have to appear further [when it is already everywhere already]? 'He did not fulfill the Buddhist Path' in that a buddha [is already a buddha, so he] does not have to become one again. An ancient said: 'Buddha is always in the world, but he is not stained by worldly things.'

"Good people, do you want to get to be a buddha? Do not follow the myriad things. When mind is born the myriad things are born, and when mind is destroyed the myriad things are destroyed. When the one mind is unborn, the myriad things are without fault.

"In the world and beyond it, there is no Buddha and there is no Dharma, nor do they appear, nor have they ever been lost. If they exist [at all], they are all just words and names, to take in and lead along small children, medicines that are applied, obvious names and formulations. But names and formulations are not so by themselves: it is the luminous aware one in you that scans and perceives and knows and illuminates, that assigns all the names and phrases. Worthy people, only after creating all five kinds of unremitting hellish karma do you find liberation."

Someone asked: "What are the five kinds of unremitting hellish karma?"

Linji said: "Killing your father, hurting your mother, shedding a buddha's blood, disrupting the harmony of the sangha, and burning scriptures and images—these are the five kinds of acts leading to uninterrupted hell [according to the Buddhist scriptures, but in Zen there is a special sense]:

"Ignorance is the father. When in a moment of mind you find that the place where things arise and disappear is unattainable, so that you are like an echo answering the void, unconcerned wherever you are—this is called killing your father.

"Craving and desire is the mother. When in a moment of mind you enter the realm of desire seeking what you crave and only see the emptiness of all things, with no attachments anywhere—this is called hurting your mother.

"When you are in the realm of purity, if there is no moment of mind when you give rise to interpretation, so everywhere is dark—this is called shedding a buddha's blood.

"If in a moment of thought you can correctly comprehend and arrive at the emptiness and baselessness of the entanglements and impetus of vexations—this is called disrupting the harmony of the sangha.

"Seeing the emptiness of causal connections, of mind, and of phenomena, in a decisive moment you become transcendent and unconcerned—this is burning scriptures and images.

"Good people, if you can comprehend like this, you will avoid being obstructed by ordinary and holy names. [Otherwise, as usual] you interpret the empty fist as if it really held something and vainly concoct strange things among the elements of sensory experience. You slight yourselves when you bow out saying that you are only ordinary people, while those [who succeeded on the Path] were sages.

"You shaven-headed ones with many births to go, what is the big hurry? You have put on a lion's skin, yet you howl like little

foxes. You are really great people, but you do not breathe with the energy of the really great. You refuse to believe in what's in your
502c own house, and instead go seeking outside like this. You fall into traps with the empty and free names and formulations used by the ancients and try to make patterns of categories by depending on them, but you are unable to comprehend them on your own. When you encounter objects you become entangled; when you meet with sensory experiences you grasp them. Delusion arises everywhere you touch; you have no sure stability of your own.

"Good people of the Path, do not grasp what I say. Why? Because verbal explanations have no basis: they are temporary sketches on the void, like images formed of colored clouds. Good people, do not think 'Buddha' is the ultimate. I see [such dualistic views of an external buddha] as a stink-hole. [Concepts of] 'bodhisattva' and 'arhat' are fetters and chains, things to bind people with. That's why [in the stories in the sutras] Mañjuśrī slew Buddha with his sword and Aṅgulimāla took his knife and wounded Buddha. Good people, there is no buddha that can be attained. Even the three vehicles, the five categories of beings, the round and the sudden manifestations of the teachings, [and all Buddhist formulations] are all just medicines to deal with the diseases of a certain period. There is no real doctrine at all. If there are [doctrinal teachings], they are open announcements that show some semblance of [real truth], public verbal demonstrations. Arranged for effect, they explain as they do for the time being.

"Good people, there are some misguided monks who attach their efforts to what is in these teachings, trying to find a world-transcending truth, but they are making a mistake. If people seek Buddha, they lose Buddha; if they seek the Path, they lose the Path; if they seek the patriarchs, they lose the patriarchs.

"Worthy people, make no mistake about it. For now I don't care if you understand the sutras and the śāstras, I don't care if you are a prince or a high official, I don't care if your eloquence is like a waterfall, I don't care if you are intelligent and knowledgeable. All I require of you is correct understanding. Good people, even if you can interpret a hundred sutras and śāstras, you are not as good as a simple monk without concerns. You may interpret them, but it is only to put down other people—you have the victory-and-loss mentality of the asura. You are ignorant of self and others, and are increasing your hellish karma. Take for example the monk Shanxing [in the Nirvāṇa Sūtra]: he could interpret the whole canon, but he was reborn in hell—there was no room for him on earth.

"Better to have no concerns, to stop and rest. When hunger comes, eat. When sleep comes, close your eyes. Fools may laugh at us, but the wise know. Good people, do not seek in texts. Your mind moves and gets fatigued, and you breathe in cold energy that does you no good. Better to let the causal nexus be unborn for a moment, and go beyond the bodhisattvas in the provisional studies of the three vehicles.

"Worthy people, do not pass your days following routines. In the past, before I had seen, the darkness was everywhere. I could not pass the time in vain: with my guts burning and my mind agitated I ran off to seek the Path. Later I found power, and only then reached the day of enlightenment, today. When I talk with you like this, it is to urge you people of the Path not to live for [mundane things] like clothing and food. It is easy to go along looking at the world. It is hard to meet an enlightened teacher. It is like the udumbara flower, that appears once in an age.

"You have come from all over because you've heard talk of an old guy called Linji. You came to try to stump me with a question, to make me unable to say anything. But when students are exposed to me functioning with the whole essence, they open up a vacant stare and cannot move their mouths at all, they are flustered and do not know what to use to answer me.

"I say to them: Donkeys are not capable of the majestic walk of
dragons and elephants. You come from many places pointing to your 503a
breasts and saying 'I understand Zen, I understand the Path,' but
when you get here most of you cannot do anything at all. What a
shame it is that you take this body and mind around everywhere

flapping your lips, telling lies and scolding people in the village lanes. Someday [in hell] you'll be beaten with an iron club. You are not true leavers of home—you are totally in the grasp of the asura realm [of jealous competition, ambition, anger, power-seeking].

"In the Path of Perfect Truth, we do not seek stimulation in argument and debate, nor do we make a clatter to refute outsiders. The succession of buddhas and ancestral teachers has had no other intent [but truth itself]. If there are verbal teachings, these come under the category of teaching formats of the three vehicles for different categories of beings, analyses of cause and effect in the realm of humans and devas. The round, sudden teaching [of Zen] is not this way. The youth Sudhana did not seek for faults [as he journeyed and learned from various teachers on his road to enlightenment].

"Worthy people, do not misuse mind. It is a great ocean that never pauses. You carry around a dead corpse like this, but you intend to go all over the world. You create for yourselves barriers of opinion and perception, and use them to obstruct mind.

"The sun [of enlightenment] is high; there are no clouds; it lights up the sky, shining everywhere. If you have no scales [of delusion] over your eyes, there are no flowers in the sky [no tricks of perception where you see things that aren't there].

"Good people, if you want to be in accord with the Dharma, just do not give rise to doubts. 'Extended, it stretches through the universe. Gathered in, there's not even a thread.' The clear distinct solitary light has never been lacking. Eyes do not see it, ears do not hear it—what is it called? An ancient said that if you call it a thing, you miss the mark. Just look for yourself: what else is there? Talk could go on forever: each of you must personally make the effort. Take care!"

Tests

Once when Huangbo went into the kitchen he asked the cook, "What are you doing?"

The cook said, "I'm cleaning the rice for the community of monks." Huangbo said, "How much do they eat in one day?"

The cook said, "About three hundred pounds."

Huangbo said, "Isn't that too much?"

The cook said, "I'm afraid it's still not enough."

Huangbo then hit him.

The cook left and told Linji about this. Linji said, "I will test this old fellow for you." As soon as Linji came to attend on Huangbo, Huangbo recounted the story.

Linji said, "The cook did not understand. Please, Master, let me turn a word on his behalf." Linji then asked: "Isn't it too much?"

Huangbo said, "Why not say, 'Tomorrow we'll eat another load'?" Linji said, "What do you mean, tomorrow? We'll eat it right now." Then he slapped Huangbo.

Huangbo said, "This crazy guy has come again to pluck the tiger's whiskers."

Linji then shouted and left.

Later Guishan asked Yangshan, "What did these two venerable adepts mean [in this interchange]?"

Yangshan said, "What do you say, Master?"

Guishan said, "Only when you raise a child do you come to realize your father's benevolence."

Yangshan said, "Not so."

Guishan said, "What do you say?"

Yangshan said, "It's like bringing in a thief who ransacks your house."

Linji asked a monk, "Where do you come from?" The monk immediately shouted. Linji saluted him and sat down. The monk hesitated trying to think what to do. Linji hit him.

Linji saw a monk coming so he held his whisk upright. The
monk bowed, and then Linji hit him. 503b

He saw another monk coming and again held the whisk upright. The monk paid no attention. Linji also hit him.

When Linji met Puhua, he said to him, "When I sent an express letter from the south to Guishan, I already knew you were here waiting for me to come. Now I have come to get your help. I want to set up the school of Huangbo now. You have to help me consolidate [my gains] and get rid of [my faults]." Puhua bid Linji take care and departed.

Later Kefu came and Linji asked him the same thing. Kefu too bade farewell and left.

Three days later, Puhua returned and inquired of Linji, "What were you saying the other day?" Linji picked up a cudgel and drove him out with blows.

After another three days, Kefu too came back and asked Linji, "Why did you beat Puhua the other day?" Linji again picked up a cudgel and drove him out with blows.

One day Linji was attending a vegetarian feast at a donor's house with Puhua. Linji asked Puhua, "A single hair swallows the giant ocean, and a mustard seed contains Mt. Sumeru. Is this the wondrous function of spiritual powers, or is it fundamentally in essence so?" Puhua kicked over the table the food was on. Linji said, "Too crude." Puhua said, "What place is this to talk of crude or fine?"

The next day Linji again went to the [ongoing] vegetarian feast with Puhua. He asked Puhua, "How are today's offerings like yesterday's?" As before, Puhua kicked over the table of food. Linji said, "You're right of course, but too crude." Puhua said, "You blind man! What crude or fine does the Buddha Dharma talk about?" Linji then stuck out his tongue.

One day Linji was sitting with Heyang and Muta by the stove in the monks' hall. They were talking about Puhua, who was in the marketplace every day capering around acting crazy, and wondering whether he was an ordinary man or a sage.

Before their talk finished, Puhua came in, so Linji asked him, "Are you an ordinary man or a sage?" Puhua said, "You tell me, am I an ordinary man or a sage?" Linji then shouted.

Puhua pointed to them and said, "Heyang is a new bride, Muta is an old lady. Linji is a little pisser, but he has the eye." Linji said, "You thief!" Puhua cried, "Thief! Thief!" and went out.

One day Puhua was in front of the monks' hall, eating some raw vegetables. Linji saw him and said, "Just like a donkey." Puhua made a donkey's bray. Linji said, "You thief!" Puhua cried, "Thief! Thief!" and went out.

Every day in the marketplace Puhua would ring a bell and said, "If you come in light, I hit you in light; if you come in darkness, I hit you in darkness. If you come from all sides, I hit you like a whirlwind. If you come from emptiness, I hit you with blows one after another."

Linji sent his attendant [with instructions] to hold Puhua fast as soon as he saw him talk like this and say, "If I don't come in any of these ways, then what?" [When the attendant did this] Puhua pushed him away and said, "Tomorrow there's a feast at the Temple of Great Compassion."

The attendant returned and related this to Linji. Linji said, "I'd always doubted this guy."

There was an experienced elder who came to study with Linji. He asked, "Should I bow or not?" Linji shouted. The elder then bowed. Linji said, "A fine petty thief!" The elder said, "Thief! Thief!" then left. Linji said, "Better not mention having no concerns."

Linji asked the head monk who was standing right there, "Was
there fault or not?" The head monk said, "There was." Linji said,
"Was it the guest or the host who was at fault?" The head monk
said, "Both were at fault." Linji said, "Where did the fault lie?"
The head monk then went out. Linji said, "Better not mention 503c
having no concerns."

Later a monk took up [this incident] with Nanquan. Nanquan said, "Two prime steeds prancing together."

Once Linji went to an army camp to attend a vegetarian feast. At the gate he met the officers. He pointed to a pillar that was there and asked, "Is it ordinary or holy?" The officers said nothing. Linji struck the pillar and said, "Even if you could say something, it's still just a wooden post." Then he went in.

Linji asked a monk in charge of temple property, "Where have you come from?"

The supervisor-monk said, "I travel back and forth in the prefecture selling rice."

Linji said, "Have you sold it all?"

The supervisor-monk said, "I have sold it all."

Linji took his staff and drew a line in front of him and said, "Have you sold this one?"

The supervisor-monk shouted, and then Linji hit him.

The monk in charge of the scriptures came. Linji told him what had been said. The monk in charge of the scriptures said, "The supervisor-monk does not understand what you mean, Master." Linji said, "What about you?" The monk in charge of the scriptures then bowed, and Linji hit him too.

When a lecturer-monk came to meet with him, Linji asked, "What sutras and śāstras do you expound?"

The lecturer said, "In a crude way, I have learned hundreds of Buddhist treatises."

Linji said, "There's one person who clearly understands the whole canon. There's another person who cannot understand the whole canon. Are they the same or different?"

The lecturer said, "If you clearly understand, they are the same. If you cannot understand, they are different."

Lepu, the attendant, was standing behind Linji and said, "Lecturer, what place is this to talk of the same and different?"

Linji turned around and asked Lepu, "What about you, attendant?" Lepu then shouted.

After Linji had seen the lecturer-monk off and come back, he asked Lepu, "Just now, were you shouting at me?" When Lepu said yes, Linji hit him.

Linji heard that Deshan the second generation teacher had said, "If you can speak, thirty blows. If you cannot speak, thirty blows." Linji sent Lepu there [with instructions] to ask him, "Why thirty blows if I can speak?" Lepu was to wait until Deshan was about to hit him, then grab the staff and give it a pull, to see how Deshan would act.

When Lepu got there, he questioned Deshan as he had been instructed. Deshan then hit him, and Lepu held onto the staff and gave a pull. Deshan then returned to the abbot's room.

Lepu returned and told Linji what had happened. Linji said, "I had always doubted this old fellow. Nevertheless, did you see Deshan?"

As Lepu tried to think of what to say, Linji hit him.

One day [the Buddhist layman and superintendent of Henanfu] Wang Jingchu paid a visit to Linji. He was with Linji observing things in front of the monks' hall, when he asked, "Do the monks in this hall read the sutras?" Linji said, "They don't read the sutras." Wang asked, "Do they study Zen?" Linji said, "They don't study Zen."

Wang said, "If they don't read the sutras and don't study Zen, ultimately what are they doing?" Linji said, "We're making them all
into buddhas and patriarchs." Wang said, "Though gold dust is valu- 504a
able, when it falls in the eye it blurs the vision. What about that?" Linji said, "I thought you were an ordinary conventional fellow."

Linji asked Xingshan, "What is the white ox on open ground?" Xingshan said, "Moo, moo." Linji said, "Are you mute?" Xingshan said, "What about you, elder?" Linji said, "You animal!"

Linji asked Lepu, "Since ancient times, one person works with blows, and one person works with shouts. Which is more intimate?"

Lepu said, "Neither is intimate."

Linji said, "What is intimacy?"

Lepu shouted. At that Linji hit him.

Linji saw a monk coming and extended both hands. The monk said nothing. Linji said, "Do you understand?" [The monk replied,] "I don't understand." Linji said, "The undifferentiated whole cannot be split apart. I give you two cents."

Dajue came to study with Linji. Linji held up his whisk. Dajue spread out his mat. Linji threw down the whisk. Dajue rolled up the mat and entered the monks' hall.

All the other monks said, "Is this monk an old friend of our master's? He didn't bow, and yet he was not beaten."

When Linji heard of this, he had Dajue summoned. When Dajue appeared, Linji said, "Everyone is saying that you have never studied with an elder like me before." Dajue said, "I don't know," and then on his own joined the congregation.

In the course of his travels, Zhaozhou studied with Linji. He met Linji as he was washing his feet, and asked him, "What is the meaning of the Patriarch coming from the west?"

Linji said, "Right now it so happens I am washing my feet."

Zhaozhou approached Linji and made a gesture of listening.

Linji said, "You're demanding to be splashed with a second ladleful of dirty water."

Zhaozhou then left.

There was a certain advanced monk named Ding who came to study with Linji. He asked, "What is the great meaning of the Buddha Dharma?" Linji got off his bench, held Ding fast, and gave him a slap, then pushed him away. For a long time Ding just stood there.

A monk who was looking on said, "Elder Ding, why don't you bow?" Only then did Ding bow—suddenly he was greatly enlightened.

Magu came to study with Linji. He spread out his sitting mat and asked, "On Twelve-Faced Guanyin, which is the correct face?"

Linji got off his bench: with one hand he picked up the sitting mat, and with the other hand he grabbed Magu, saying, "Where has Twelve-Faced Guanyin gone?"

Magu turned around and tried to sit on the bench. Linji picked up his staff and hit him. Magu took it from him and they pulled each other into the abbot's room.

Linji questioned a monk: "Sometimes a shout is like the diamond king's precious sword. Sometimes a shout is like a golden-haired lion crouching on the ground. Sometimes a shout is like a probing pole and a shade used in fishing to look below the surface of the water. Sometimes a shout does not function as a shout. How do you understand this?" As the monk tried to think of what to say, Linji shouted.

Linji asked a nun, "Do you come from good or from evil?" The 504b
nun shouted. Linji picked up his staff and said, "Say more, say more." The nun shouted again, so Linji hit her.

Longya asked, "What is the meaning of the Patriarch coming from the West?"

Linji said, "Pass me the back brace."

Longya handed the back brace to Linji, who took it and hit him with it. Longya said, "Go ahead and hit me. In essence there is no such meaning."

Later Longya went to Cuiwei and asked, "What is the meaning of the Patriarch coming from the west?"

Cuiwei said, "Pass me the cushion."

Longya handed the cushion to Cuiwei, who took it and hit him with it. Longya said, "Go ahead and hit me. In essence there is no such meaning."

Later when Longya was staying at a temple [teaching], there was a monk who entered his room to ask for instruction. [The monk asked,] "Master, when you were on your travels, and you studied with those two venerable adepts, did you approve of them or not?" Longya said, "As far as that goes, I deeply approved, but in essence there is no meaning of the Patriarch coming from the west."

There was a congregation of five hundred on Mt. Jingshan, but few sought instruction [from the teacher there.] Huangbo directed Linji to go to Jingshan, saying to him, "How will you act when you get there?" Linji said, "When I arrive there, expedient methods will appear by themselves."

When Linji got to Jingshan, he went up to the teaching hall with his robe still tied up for travelling and saw the teacher. When the teacher lifted his head, Linji gave a shout. As the teacher tried to open his mouth, Linji shook out his sleeves and left.

Shortly afterwards a monk asked the teacher, "What did that monk just now have to say, that he shouted at you, Master?" The teacher said, "This monk comes from Huangbo's assembly. If you want to know, better ask him." After this the greater part of the congregation of five hundred on Mt. Jingshan dispersed and went their separate ways.

One day Puhua kept going up to people in the market streets and asking them for a monk's garment. People all offered him garments, but Puhua didn't want any of them.

[Meanwhile] Linji ordered the supervisor-monk to buy a coffin. When Puhua returned, Linji said to him, "I've made a monk's garment for you." Puhua then lifted the coffin up onto his shoulder and went around the market streets calling out, "Linji has made me a monk's garment! I'm going over to the east gate to die."

The people in the market all crowded around and followed him to watch this. [But when they got to the east gate] Puhua said, "Today I'm not ready yet. Tomorrow I'll go to the south gate and die."

This went on for three days until no one believed him any more. On the fourth day nobody followed him to watch. Alone, Puhua went outside the city walls, climbed into the coffin, and asked a passerby to nail it shut and spread a cloth over it.

[As the news of this spread] the townspeople all came running to open the coffin. [When they opened it] the body had vanished. There was just the sound of a bell heard in the air, growing fainter and fainter as it moved away.

Conduct

Early on, when Linji was in Huangbo's assembly, his conduct was pure and unified. The head monk exclaimed, "Though he is younger, he is different from the rest of the congregation." So he asked
504c Linji how long he had been there. Linji said three years. The head monk said, "Have you ever asked Huangbo anything?" Linji said, "Never. I wouldn't know what to ask." The head monk said, "Why don't you go ask the Master in the teaching hall what is the true meaning of the Buddha Dharma?" Linji went and asked, but before he had finished talking, Huangbo hit him.

Linji went back to the head monk who asked, "How did your question go?" Linji said, "Before I finished talking, the Master hit me. I don't understand." The head monk said, "Just go ask again." Linji went again to ask, and again Huangbo hit him. Three times Linji asked like this, and three times he got hit.

Linji came back and told the head monk, "I had the good fortune to meet with your compassion, and you directed me to ask the Master a question. Three times I asked, and three times I got hit. I regret that my karmic barriers are such that I do not understand the profound meaning of this. Now I am going away." The head monk said, "When you go, you have to say goodbye to the Master." Linji bowed and withdrew.

The head monk went ahead of him to the Master's room and said to Huangbo, "This young guy asking questions is very much in accord with the Dharma. When he comes to say goodbye, please use expedient means to receive him, and give him some further explanations, so he will become a great tree giving shade to the world's people."

When Linji came to bid farewell, Huangbo said, "Don't go anywhere else but to Dayu's place on the shore at Gaoan. He will surely explain for you."

When Linji got there, Dayu asked, "Where have you come from?" Linji said, "From Huangbo's place." Dayu said, "What did Huangbo have to say?" Linji said, "Three times I asked about the true meaning of the Buddha Dharma, and three times I got hit. I don't know if I was at fault or not." Dayu said, "Huangbo was so kind, he wore himself out for you, but you still come here asking whether there was fault or not!"

At these words, Linji was greatly enlightened and said, "Actually there's not much to Huangbo's Buddha Dharma."

Dayu held him tight and said, "You bed-wetting little devil! A little while ago you were talking about whether you were at fault or not, and yet now you say that there's not much to Huangbo's Buddha Dharma. What truth have you seen? Speak quickly!"

Linji punched Dayu three times in the ribs. Dayu pushed him off and said, "Your teacher is Huangbo. It's none of my business." Linji said goodbye to Dayu and went back to Huangbo.

When Huangbo saw him coming he said, "This fellow comes and goes again and again—when will he ever be finished?" Linji said, "It's all due to your extreme kindness," and after saluting Huangbo, stood there attending on him.

Huangbo asked, "Where have you come from?" Linji said,
"Yesterday I carried out your merciful instructions to go see Dayu,
and now I've come back." Huangbo said, "What did Dayu have to
say?" Linji recounted what had happened. Huangbo said, "Why
does this guy come here—is he waiting for a sound beating?" Linji
said, "What do you mean, waiting? Have it right now," and then
505a he slapped Huangbo. Huangbo said, "This crazy guy has come
back again to pluck the tiger's whiskers." Linji then shouted.
Huangbo said, "Attendant, lead this crazy man back to the hall."

Later Guishan brought this story up to Yangshan to question him. He asked Yangshan, "At the time, did Linji get Dayu's power or Huangbo's power?" Yangshan said, "Not only did he ride the tiger's head, he also was able to hold the tiger's tail."

Once Linji was planting some pine trees. Huangbo asked, "Why are you planting so many trees here deep in the mountains?" Linji said, "First, I'm improving the scenery around the monastery. Second, I'm making a sign for later people." Having said that, he took his mattock and hit the ground three times. Huangbo said, "Even so, you have already taken thirty blows from me." Linji again hit the ground with his mattock three times, with a long exhalation of breath in mock fear. Huangbo said, "With you, our school will flourish greatly in the world."

Later Guishan brought up this story and asked Yangshan, "Did Huangbo only entrust his teaching to Linji, or were there others?" Yangshan said, "There were others, but that was so long ago I don't want to mention them to you, Master." [Linji and Guishan were near contemporaries.]

Guishan said, "Nevertheless, I still want to know. Just mention them so I can see." Yangshan said, "One man pointed south, and the imperative was carried out throughout the southeast. It will meet with a great wind [in the person of Fengxue, 'Wind Cave,' a successor of Linji in the third generation] and lapse."

Once when Linji was attending on Deshan, Deshan said, "I'm tired today." Linji said, "Why is this old guy talking in his sleep?" Deshan then hit him. Linji turned over the bench. Deshan let it go at that.

Once during the general call to labor Linji was hoeing the ground. When he saw Huangbo coming, he stood there holding his hoe. Huangbo said, "Is this guy tired?" Linji said, "He hasn't even lifted his hoe—tired of what?" Huangbo then hit him. Linji grabbed the staff and pulled Huangbo down by it.

Huangbo called to the duty-distributor, "Help me up!" The duty-distributor came forward to help him up and said, "Why do you tolerate the insolence of this crazy fellow, Master?" As soon as Huangbo got up, he hit the duty-distributor.

Linji hoed the ground and said, "Everywhere else they cremate with fire. Here we bury them alive for a time."

Later Guishan asked Yangshan, "What did Huangbo mean when he hit the duty-distributor?" Yangshan said, "The true thief escaped, so the ones sent after him took the beating."

One day Linji was sitting in front of the monks' hall. When he saw Huangbo coming, he closed his eyes. Huangbo made a gesture of fright, and returned to the abbot's room. Linji followed him back to the abbot's room to bow in thanks.

The head monk was in attendance on Huangbo at the time. Huangbo said, "Though this monk is young, he knows that this business exists." The head monk said, "Master, your feet aren't touching the ground if you certify this young man." Huangbo hit himself on the mouth. The head monk said, "As long as you know."

Linji was in the hall asleep when Huangbo came down to see him. Huangbo rapped on the sounding board with his staff. Linji 505b raised his head, saw it was Huangbo, and went back to sleep. Huangbo hit the sounding board again and went back to the quarters of the senior monks. When he saw the head monk he said, "Down in the hall that young guy is really sitting in meditation. Why are you here engaged in false thought?" The head monk said, "What is the old guy doing?" Huangbo hit the sounding board and went out.

Later Guishan asked Yangshan, "What was Huangbo's intention when he went into the monks' hall?" Yangshan said, "Two winning faces on a single die."

One day during the general call to labor, Linji was walking behind everyone else [as they all went out to work in the gardens.] Huangbo turned back and saw him empty-handed and said, "Where is your hoe?" Linji said, "Someone took it away." Huangbo said, "Come over here, I want to talk to you about something." When Linji approached, Huangbo held his hoe upright and said, "No one in the world can pick this one up." Linji pulled it into his own hand, held it upright, and said, "Then why is it in my hand?" Huangbo said, "Today we've had a great call to labor indeed!" Then he went back to the monastery.

Later Guishan asked Yangshan, "The hoe was in Huangbo's hand: why was it taken away by Linji?" Yangshan said, "The thief is a nobody, a small man, but he knows more than a gentleman-sage, a lord's son."

Linji went to deliver a letter from Huangbo to Guishan. At the time, Yangshan was in charge of receiving travellers [at Guishan's place]. He accepted the letter, then asked Linji, "This is Huangbo's. Which is yours, messenger?" Linji then slapped him. Yangshan held him fast and said, "Brother, since you know about this business, let's stop at that."

Together they went to see Guishan. Guishan asked, "How many are there in the congregation with brother Huangbo?" Linji said, "Seven hundred." Guishan said, "Who is their guide?" Linji said, "He just sent you a letter."

Then Linji asked Guishan in return, "How many in the congregation here with you, Master?" Guishan said, "Fifteen hundred." Linji said, "Too many." Guishan said, "Brother Huangbo is not short of them either."

Linji bade farewell to Guishan and Yangshan went along to see him off. Yangshan told him, "Later, go north, and there will be a place to stay." Linji said, "How could there be such a thing?" Yangshan said, "Just go. Later there will be someone to assist you there, brother. This man will have a head but no tail, a beginning but no end."

Later when Linji came to Zhenzhou [in northeast China] Puhua was already there. When Linji appeared in the world [to teach], Puhua helped him. Before Linji had been there very long, Puhua completely vanished.

Linji climbed Mt. Huangbo in the middle of the summer. He saw the master there [himself called Huangbo] reading a sutra. Linji said, "I thought you were an enlightened man, but actually you are only an old monk gleaning from books."

After staying several days, Linji said farewell and left. Huangbo said to him, "You came interrupting the summer [period of practice] and now you leave before the summer is over." Linji said, "I was
paying my respects to you for a while, Master." Huangbo then drove 505c
him out with blows. After walking a few miles, Linji was full of doubts about this event, so he returned and finished out the summer.

One day Linji said goodbye to Huangbo. Huangbo asked, "Where are you going?" Linji said, "If not south of the river, then north of the river." Huangbo then hit him. Linji held him fast and gave him a slap. Huangbo laughed loudly and called to his attendant, "Bring out my late master Baizhang's back rest and table." Linji said, "Attendant, bring fire!" Huangbo said, "Even though it is so, just take them. Later you will cut off the tongues of everyone in the world."

Later Guishan asked Yangshan, "Didn't Linji turn his back on Huangbo?" Yangshan said, "Not so." Guishan said, "What do you think?" Yangshan said, "Only if you are aware of the benevolence can you repay the benevolence." Guishan said, "Are there
any cases since ancient times similar to this?" Yangshan said, 506a

"There are, but it was so long ago I don't want to mention it to you, Master." Guishan said, "I want to know anyway. Mention them so I can see." Yangshan said, "At the Śūraṅgama assembly Ānanda praised Buddha saying, 'Serving in countless lands with this profound mind is called repaying the benevolence of the buddhas.' Isn't this an instance of repaying benevolence?" Guishan said, "That's right, that's right. If your views equal your teacher's, you decrease his virtue by half. Only if your views go beyond your teacher's are you worthy to pass on the transmission."

Linji went to Bodhidharma's Stupa [at Bear Ear Mountain in Henan]. The keeper of the stupa asked him, "Elder, do you bow to buddhas or patriarchs first?" Linji said, "I do not bow to either." The keeper of the stupa said, "How can the buddhas and patriarchs be your enemies?" Linji shook out his sleeves and left.

In the course of his travels, Linji came to Longguang. Longguang was in the teaching hall and Linji came forward and asked, "How do you win victory without extending sharp pointed blades?" Longguang stayed seated. Linji said, "You are a great enlightened teacher. How can you have no expedient means?" Longguang glared at him and grunted in surprise. Linji pointed to him and said, "Today this old fellow has met defeat."

Linji went to Sanfeng. Master Ping asked, "Where do you come from?" Linji said, "From Huangbo." Ping said, "What does Huangbo say?" Linji said, "Last night the golden ox was smeared with charcoal, and up till now we've seen no trace of him." Ping said, "When the golden wind blows through the jade pipe, who knows the sound?" Linji said, "Penetrating straight through ten thousand layers of barriers, not staying in the pure empyrean." Ping said, "This question of yours is too lofty." Linji said, "The dragon gives birth to a golden phoenix, which smashes through the blue crystal [vault of heaven]." Ping said, "Sit awhile and eat some vegetables." He asked Linji, "Where have you just come here from?" Linji said, "From Longguang." Ping said, "How is Longguang these days?" Linji left.

Linji came to Daci. Daci was sitting in the abbot's room. Linji asked, "How is it when staying upright in the abbot's room?" Daci said, "The cold pine is one color, a thousand years are different. The old countryman picks a flower and it's spring in ten thousand lands." Linji said, "The essential body of perfect wisdom transcends modern and ancient. The three mountains [of the immortals] lock off the ten thousand barriers." Daci then shouted, and Linji shouted too. Daci said, "What?" Linji shook out his sleeves and left.

Linji came to Huayan's place in Rangzhou. Huayan was leaning on his staff in a sleeping pose. Linji said, "Why are you asleep, Master?" Huayan said, "An expert Zen traveller looks the same but isn't." Linji said, "Attendant, bring a pot of tea for the Master to drink." Huayan called to the duty-distributor, "Put this monk in the third seat."

Linji came to Cuiyan. Cuiyan asked, "Where do you come from?" Linji said, "From Huangbo." Cuiyan said, "What does Huangbo say
to instruct people?" Linji said, "Huangbo says nothing." Cuiyan said, 506b
"Why not?" Linji said, "If he did, there would be no way to mention it." Cuiyan said, "Just go ahead and mention it so I can see." Linji said, "A single arrow flies past India."

Linji came to Xiangtian and asked him, "It's not ordinary and it's not holy. Please, teacher, speak quickly." Xiangtian said, "I am only thus." Linji gave a shout and said, "What are so many monks looking for here?"

Linji came to Minghua. Minghua asked, "Why do you keep coming and going back and forth?" Linji said, "I'm just wearing out straw sandals in vain." Minghua said, "But ultimately, what for?" Linji said, "This old guy does not even recognize a Zen saying."

On the road on the way to Fenglin, Linji met an old woman. She asked, "Where are you going?" Linji said, "To Fenglin." The old woman said, "At the moment Fenglin is not there." Linji said, "Where did he go?" The old woman walked off. Linji called to her, and when she turned her head back, Linji hit her.

When he arrived, Fenglin asked, "Is there anything you want to ask about?" Linji said, "Why cut a wound into the flesh?" Fenglin said, "The moon over the ocean is clear, without reflections, but the swimming fish is deluding himself." Linji said, "Since the moon over the ocean has no reflections, how could the swimming fish be deluded?" Fenglin said, "Observing the wind, we know waves will arise. We play over the waters, wild sails billowing in the wind." Linji said, "The solitary orb shines alone, rivers and mountains are still. At the sound of a spontaneous laugh, heaven and earth are startled." Fenglin said, "Go ahead and light up heaven and earth with your tongue. Try to say a phrase that matches the potential of this moment so I can see [if you can]." Linji said, "When you meet a master swordsman on the road, you must show your sword. Don't show your verses unless to a poet." Fenglin stopped at that. Linji then gave a verse:

There's nothing like the Great Path
Whichever way you go.
Even sparks struck from stone cannot overtake it.
Even lightning cannot penetrate it.

Guishan asked Yangshan, "Since even sparks struck from stone cannot overtake it, and even lightning cannot penetrate it, what have all the sages since antiquity used in order to function as [enlightened] people?" Yangshan said, "What do you mean, Master?" Guishan said, "There's only words and talk, no real meaning at all." Yangshan said, "Not so." Guishan said, "Then what do you think?" Yangshan said, "Officially, not even a needle is allowed in, but unofficially even a horse and cart can get through."

Linji went to Jinniu. When Jinniu saw him coming, he held his staff horizontal, and crouched in the gateway. Linji hit the staff with his hand three times, then turned away and went back to the hall, where he sat in the first seat. When Jinniu came and saw him, he asked, "When guest and host meet, each has majestic deportment. Where do you come from that you are so impolite?" Linji said, "What did you say, old Master?" As Jinniu was about to open his mouth, Linji hit him. Jinniu then made as if to fall. Linji
506c hit him again. Jinniu said, "This is not right for today."

Guishan asked Yangshan, "Was there victory and defeat between these two venerable adepts or not?" Yangshan said, "If they win, they both win; if they lose, they both lose."

When Linji was about to die, he took his teacher's seat and said, "After my demise, you must not destroy the treasury of my eye for the true Dharma." Sansheng came forward and said, "How could we dare to destroy the treasury of your correct Dharma eye, Master?"

Linji said, "Later, when people ask you questions, what will you say?" Sansheng gave a shout.

Linji said, "Who would have known that my eye for the true Dharma would perish with this blind donkey?" As his words ended, he died sitting upright.

Wumen's Gate

Translated from the Chinese
Taishō Volume 48, Number 2005

by

J. C. Cleary

Translator's Introduction

The *Wu Men Guan* (Wumen's gate, or the Barrier of the gate of nothingness) is a classic collection of forty-eight Zen "public cases" (Jp. *kōan*, Ch. *gong an*) accompanied by comments and verses, presented as teaching materials within the Zen tradition. Zen students would focus their attention on these cases and meditate via their intricate patterns of meaning. By interrupting and reshaping patterns of thought, these classic Zen cases were intended as tools to refine minds and open them to wider perspectives on reality. For those who care to follow their imagery and logic, they present timeless scenes, concentrated demonstrations of Buddhist truth, glimpses of the life of wisdom.

Over the years in Zen communities, stories of the sayings and doings of the great early masters provided themes for teaching Buddhist principles and were also used as focal points in meditation. Being widely known in the Zen communities, they were indeed "public cases." As objects of discussion and study, in time the public cases became surrounded by a rich lore of responses, verses of praise, pointers, and comments, some of which in turn became famous remarks and gestures subject to further comment.

Going on for centuries, this world of Zen koan discourse became exceedingly refined, intricate, and subtle. The classic collections of Zen public cases and commentaries like the *Blue Cliff Record* and the *Book of Equanimity* were produced in the twelfth century, and many similarly inspired collections appeared thereafter. The *Wu Men Guan* is from the mid-thirteenth century. Its many-layered meanings lie within a very highly polished and dense style that can be abrupt and unapproachable and disconcerting. The author Wumen Huikai was talking about stories his audience knew by heart and had chewed over if not digested. Hence he could be terse and move quickly between levels.

The *Wu Men Guan* has been venerated and regarded as a masterpiece in East Asian Zen circles ever since its appearance. Many have savored its verbal brilliance, have meditated on its patterns, and have taken it as a test of their Zen insight. With this English translation we hope that interested Western readers will gain access to Wumen's Gate.

Preface by Chengsun

Explain the Path with no gate, and everyone in the world can enter. Explain the Path with a gate, and you are not qualified to be a teacher. To impose a few footnotes at the outset seems like putting on a rain hat over another rain hat. To insist that I praise [Wumen] is like trying to squeeze juice out of dry bamboo. To write out these howls is basically not worth my tossing them down. Since I have thrown them down, don't let even a drop fall into the rivers and lakes. Even the fastest jet-black steed cannot catch up. 292b

First year of the Shao Ding era [1228], last day of the seventh month. Written by Chengsun of Xi-an.

Preface by Huikai

On the fifth day of the first month of the second year of the Shao Ding era we respectfully observe the Imperial Birthday. On the fifth day of the twelfth month of last year, [His Majesty's] subject the monk [Wumen] Huikai had printed and circulated [a collection of] forty-eight cases citing the enlightenment stories of the Buddhas and Patriarchs. We dedicate this to extending the longevity of our present Supreme Imperial Majesty's sage person: may he live ten thousand years, and ten thousand times ten thousand years! We humbly hope that His Imperial Majesty's sagely illumination may equal the sun and moon and that his farseeing plans may equal heaven and earth. From all directions the people will acclaim their Lord for having the Path, and all the world will rejoice in his civilizing influence that has no [forced] action.

Respectfully spoken by Huikai, the monk and subject of His Majesty, who acts as abbot and transmits the Dharma at the Baoen Youci Zen Temple [founded by] the merit of the Empress Ciyi.

Preface

For the Buddha's words, the mind is the source: the gate of nothingness is the gate to truth.

Since it is the gate of nothingness, how can we enter? Surely you have read the saying, "What comes in through the gate is not the family jewels; what is gained from causal circumstances is bound to decay."

Such talk is like raising waves where there is no wind, like cutting a wound in healthy flesh. But even worse is to get stuck on words and phrases in the search for interpretative understanding: [this is like] trying to hit the moon with a stick [or] scratching an itch from outside the boot. What connection will there be?

In the summer of 1228, Huikai was head of the congregation at Longxiang at Dongjia. The patch-robed ones asked for instruction, so he took the public cases of the people of old to use as [one would use] a piece of tile to knock on a gate. He guided students according to their potentials and the potentials of the moment. Finally Huikai's remarks were copied and on the spur of the moment made into a collection of forty-eight cases, not arranged in the order he gave them. The whole collection is called *Wu Men Guan* [Wumen's barrier or The barrier of the gate of nothingness].

If you are a person [true to your real identity], you will not mind the danger; you will enter directly at a single stroke. Fearsome monsters cannot hold you back, and even the Zen Patriarchs of India and China can only beg for their lives as they look to your awesome presence. But if you hesitate, it will be like watching through a window as horse and rider go by—a blink of an eye and they've already gone past.

Verse

The Great Path, the gate of nothingness, has no gate.
Amidst the thousand differences, there is a road.
If you can pass through this barrier,
You walk alone through heaven and earth.

Case 1. Zhaozhou's Dog

A monk asked Zhaozhou, "Does a dog have the Buddha nature or not?"

Zhaozhou said, "No."

Wumen said,

To study Zen you must pass through the barrier of the Buddhas and Patriarchs. For wondrous enlightenment you must get to the end of the road of the mind. If you do not penetrate the ancestral teachers' barrier, if you do not end the road of the mind, then in all that you do [seeking to follow the Buddhist Path] you are but a ghost haunting the forests and fields.

But tell me, what is the barrier of the Buddhas and Patriarchs? It is this one word "No"—this is the barrier of Zen. This is why [this collection] is called the Zen school's barrier of the gate of No. If you can pass through it, not only will you see Zhaozhou in person but you will then be
able to walk together hand in hand with all the generations 293a
of ancestral teachers. You will join eyebrows with the ancestral teachers, see through the same eyes, and hear through the same ears. Won't you be happy!

Do any of you want to pass through the barrier? Just arouse a mass of doubt throughout your whole body, extending through your three hundred sixty bones and your eighty-four thousand pores, as you come to grips with this word "No." Bring it up and keep your attention on it day and night. Don't understand it as empty nothingness, and don't understand it in terms of being and non-being. It should be as if you have swallowed a red hot iron ball that you cannot spit out. After a long time [at this] you become fully pure and ripe; inner and outer are spontaneously fused into one. It is like being a mute and having a dream: you can only know it for yourself.

Suddenly it comes forth, shaking heaven and earth. It is like taking a great commanding general's sword in your hand: you slay Buddhas and Patriarchs as you meet them. On the shore of birth and death, you find great sovereign independence; you wander at play in *samādhi* among all orders of beings in all planes of existence.

But how will you bring up [Zhaozhou's "No"] and keep your attention on it? Bring up the word "No" with your whole life force. If you do this properly without interruption, it is like a lamp of truth: once lit, it shines.

Verse

A dog . . . the Buddha nature . . .
He fully expresses the correct imperative.
As soon as you step into being and nothingness,
You lose your body and your life.

Case 2. Baizhang's Wild Fox

Every time Baizhang taught there was an old man who followed along with the congregation to hear the Dharma and left when the congregation withdrew. Unexpectedly one day he stayed behind, so Baizhang asked him, "Who is the one who stands before me?"

The old man said, "I am not human. In the time of the ancient Buddha Kāśyapa, when I was dwelling here on this mountain, a student asked me if a person of great practice still falls into cause and effect or not. I replied that he does not fall into cause and effect, and consequently I have had five hundred births in the body of a wild fox. Now I am asking you, Master, to turn a word on my behalf so that I can escape from being a wild fox." Then he asked Baizhang, "Does a person of great practice still fall into cause and effect or not?"

Baizhang said, "He is not deluded about cause and effect."

At these words the old man was greatly enlightened. He bowed in homage and said, "I have already shed the fox's body, which rests on the other side of the mountain. Please, Master, give it the funeral services due a dead monk."

Baizhang ordered the duty distributor to pound the gavel [to summon the assembly] and announced to them, "After we eat, we shall hold a funeral for a dead monk." The congregation [were puzzled] and began to discuss the matter among themselves. They went to the infirmary, but there was no one there sick. [They wondered] why Baizhang was acting like this.

After their meal, Baizhang led the congregation to a cliffside on the other side of the mountain, where he took a stick and pulled out the body of a dead fox [from a crevice in the rocks]. They then formally cremated the body.

That night Baizhang went up to the teaching hall and related the full story of what had happened.

Huangbo then asked, "One wrong reply and this man of old fell into a wild fox's body for five hundred lifetimes. If each and 293b
every reply is right, then what?"

Baizhang said, "Come here and tell him." Huangbo then came up and gave Baizhang a slap. Baizhang clapped his hands and laughed and said, "I knew barbarians' beards were red, and here's another red-bearded barbarian."

Wumen said,

[When the wild fox monk asserted that the person of great practice] "does not fall into cause and effect," why did he fall into a wild fox's body?

[When he heard that such a person] "is not deluded by cause and effect," why did he shed the fox's body? If you can focus the eye [of enlightened insight] here on this, then you will know why, long ago on Baizhang Mountain, [the old man] won for himself five hundred lifetimes flowing with the wind.

Verse

Not falling into, not being deluded by—
Two faces of a single die.
Not being deluded by, not falling into—
A thousand thousand errors.

Case 3. Judi Holds Up a Finger

Whenever he was questioned, Master Judi would just hold up a finger.

Later one of the boys [in the congregation] was asked by an outsider, "What is the essential teaching of your master?" The boy also held up a finger.

When Judi heard about this, he took a knife and cut off the boy's finger. As the boy ran out howling in pain, Judi called him back. When the boy looked back, Judi just held up a finger. The boy was abruptly enlightened.

When Judi was about to die, he told the congregation, "I got Tianlong's one-finger Zen and used it my whole life without exhausting it." As his words ended, he died.

Wumen said,

Where Judi and the boy were enlightened was not on the finger. If you can see into this, then Tianlong, Judi, the boy, and you yourself are all strung through on the same string.

Verse

Judi made a fool out of old Tianlong.
Holding up the sharp blade alone to test a little boy,
The great spirit lifts his hand without much ado
And splits apart the million layers of Flower Mountain.

Case 4. The Barbarian Has No Beard

Huoyan said, "Why does the Indian barbarian have no beard?" [Why do enlightened teachers, and the enlightened true identity within us, have no fixed, predictable characteristics by which we may recognize them?]

Wumen said,

Study must be real study. Awakening must be real awakening. For this, you must see the barbarian in person. But when I say "see in person," it has already become dualistic.

Verse

In front of fools,
We must not speak of dreams.
"The barbarian has no beard"
Adds confusion to clear wakefulness.

Case 5. Xiangyan's Up in a Tree

Master Xiangyan said, "It's like being a man up in a tree [sup- 293c
porting himself by] holding a branch between his teeth, with his hands and feet not touching the tree branches. Beneath the tree there is someone who asks about the meaning of the coming from the West [the true intent of Zen]. If he does not reply, he spurns the questioner's question. If he does reply, he perishes [by falling]. At such a moment, how should he answer?"

Wumen said,

Even if you have eloquence pouring out like a waterfall, it is totally useless [here]. Even if you can preach the whole great canon of teachings, this won't work either. If you can succeed in answering here, you bring back to life what before [for you] was a dead road [namely transcendental wisdom, your true identity], and you put to death what before was your life's path [the conventional world of conditioned consciousness]. If you cannot answer, wait for the future and ask Maitreya.

Verse

Xiangyan is a real phony;
His evil poison is endless.
Making the mouths of patch-robed monks go mute,
His whole body is squirting demon eyes.

Case 6. The World Honored One Holds Up a Flower

In ancient times, at an assembly on Spirit Mountain, the World Honored One [the Buddha] held up a flower and showed it to those gathered there.

Everyone in the assembly was silent at that moment. Only the Venerable Kāśyapa cracked a slight smile.

The World Honored One said, "I have the treasury of the Eye of the Correct Dharma, the wondrous mind of nirvana, the real formless subtle gate to Reality, the special transmission outside the scriptural teachings that does not establish texts [as sacred]. I entrust it to Mahākāśyapa."

Wumen said,

If golden-faced Gautama had had no one by his side [to understand his special meaning and smile as Kāśyapa did], he would have been forcing free men down into serfdom and selling dog meat advertised as mutton, and the assembly would have thought it was marvelous. If everyone in the assembly had smiled, how would [the Buddha] have passed on the treasury of the Eye of the Correct Dharma? If Kāśyapa had not smiled, how would [the Buddha] have passed on the treasury of the Eye of the Correct Dharma?

If you say there is transmission of the treasury of the Eye of the Correct Dharma, then old Golden-Face was lying to the ordinary people in the village lanes. If you say there is no transmission, then why did he approve only Kāśyapa?

Verse

Holding up a flower,
The tail already shows.
Kāśyapa cracks a smile,
Everyone else is helpless.

Case 7. Zhaozhou's "Wash the Bowl"

A monk asked Zhaozhou, "I have just entered the Buddhist community. I beg for your instructions, Teacher."

Zhaozhou said, "Have you eaten yet?"

The monk said, "I have eaten."

Zhaozhou said, "Then go wash the bowl." [At this] the monk had insight.

Wumen said, 294a

When Zhaozhou opens his mouth, we see his liver; he shows his heart and guts. This monk did not really listen to what was going on—he thought a bell was a jar.

Verse

Just because [Zhaozhou's answer] was so extremely clear,
It worked in reverse to make [the monk's] realization slow.
We already knew the lamp was fire—
The food has been cooked a long time already.

Case 8. The Master Cartwright Makes a Carriage

Master Yueyan asked a monk, "Xizhong [the master cartwright] made carriages [with wheels] with a hundred spokes. We roll up the two hubs and eliminate the axle: does this explain transcendence or worldly wisdom?"

Wumen said,

If you can understand directly, your eyes are like comets, your mental workings like a flash of lightning.

Verse

Where the wheel of mental workings turns,
Even those who comprehend are still deluded.
The four directions, up and down,
South, north, east, west.

Case 9. Great Pervasive Excellent Wisdom

A monk asked Master Rang of Xingyang, "The Buddha [called] Great Pervasive Excellent Wisdom sat at the site of enlightenment for ten eons, but the Buddha Dharma did not appear to him. How was it when he did not achieve the Buddha Path?"

Rang said, "This question is very fitting."

The monk said, "Since he sat at the site of enlightenment for ten eons, why did he not achieve the Buddha Path?"

Rang said, "Because he did not become a Buddha" [since he already was one].

Wumen said,

I'll only allow that the old barbarian knows, not that he understands. If an ordinary person knows, he is a sage. If a sage understands, he is an ordinary person.

Verse

Comprehending the body is not as good as comprehending the mind, then resting.
If you can comprehend the mind, the body will not be sad.
If you can comprehend both body and mind,
What need is there any more for spirit immortals to legitimize your rank?

Case 10. Qingshui, a Poor Orphan

A monk named Qingshui asked Master Caoshan, "I am a poor orphan; I beg you to succor me, Teacher."

Caoshan called to him, "Reverend Qingshui?" Qingshui responded with "Yes?"

Caoshan said, "You have drunk three bowls of our family's home-brewed Zen wine, and still you say you haven't wet your lips!"

Wumen said,

> Qingshui lost the potential of the moment; what was his mind doing then? Caoshan had the eye [of enlightenment] and profoundly judged the potentials of those who came [to him to learn]. Nevertheless, tell me, where did Reverend Qingshui drink the wine? 294b

Verse

> Poor as a destitute recluse [Fan Dan],
> Spirited as a champion of the ancient nobility [Xiang Yu],
> Though he has no way to survive,
> [Qingshui] dares to contend with [Caoshan] for the riches [of Zen].

Case 11. Zhaozhou Tests the Hermits

Zhaozhou went to a hermit's place and asked, "Is there anyone here?"

The hermit held up his fist.

Zhaozhou said, "Shallow water is not the place to moor a big ship." Then he left.

Zhaozhou went to another hermit's place and asked, "Is there anyone here?"

This hermit also held up his fist.

Zhaozhou said, "You can both capture and release, kill and bring life." Then Zhaozhou bowed to him.

Wumen said,

[Both hermits] held up their fists in the same way. Why did Zhaozhou approve one and not the other? What's so hard to understand about that?

If you can utter a turning word here, then you see that Zhaozhou's tongue is perfectly flexible. With great freedom he holds one up and puts one down. Even so, what can he do? Zhaozhou himself in his turn was exposed by the two hermits.

If you say that one hermit was better than the other, you do not have the eye to study and learn. If you say that there is no better or worse, you do not have the eye to study and learn either.

Verse

Eyes like comets,
Mental workings like lightning.
The sword that kills people:
The sword that brings people to life.

Case 12. Rui Calls His Boss

Every day Master Ruiyan would call to himself, "Boss!" Then he would answer, "Yes?" Then he would say, "Stay awake!" "I will." "From now on, don't fall for people's deceptions." "No, I won't."

Wumen said,

Old man Ruiyan is both the buyer and the seller. How many spirit heads and demon faces he brings out! Why? Away, ghosts! One that calls, one that answers, one that stays awake, one that doesn't fall for people's deceptions.

If you recognize him, you are still not right. If you imitate him, these are all wild fox views.

Verse

People studying the Path do not know the Real,
Just because they have always accepted the conscious spirit.
This, the root of birth and death for infinite eons,
Fools call the original person.

Case 13. Deshan Carries His Bowl

One day Deshan left the hall carrying his bowl. Xuefeng asked,
"The bell and drum have not yet sounded; where are you taking 294c
the bowl, old man?" Deshan then returned to the abbot's quarters.

Xuefeng described this to Yantou. Yantou said, "Deshan, who is supposedly so great, does not understand the Last Word."

When Deshan heard about this, he sent an attendant to call Yantou in. He asked Yantou, "So you don't approve of me?" Yantou tacitly indicated it was so. Deshan let it go at that.

The next day when Deshan went up to the teacher's seat, sure enough, [the way he taught] was not the same as usual. In front of the monks' hall, Yantou [was to be seen] rubbing his hands together and laughing loudly. He said, "Happily the old man does understand the Last Word. From now on, no one in the world will be able to cope with him."

Wumen said,

As for the Last Word, neither Yantou nor Deshan has ever dreamed of it. Check it out: it's like a scene in a puppet show.

Verse

If you can recognize the First Word,
Then you can understand the Last Word.
Last and First
Are not this word.

Case 14. Nanquan Kills a Cat

Once the monks from the east and west halls were arguing over a cat. Master Nanquan held up the cat and said, "If any of you can speak, you save the cat. If you cannot speak, I kill the cat." No one in the assembly could reply, so Nanquan killed the cat.

That evening Zhaozhou returned from a trip outside [the monastery]. Nanquan told him what had happened. Zhaozhou then took off his shoes, put them on top of his head, and walked out. Nanquan said, "If you had been here, you would have saved the cat."

Wumen said,

Now tell me, when Zhaozhou put his shoes on top of his head, what did he mean? If you can utter a turning word here, then you will see that Nanquan did not carry out the imperative in vain. Otherwise, danger!

Verse

If Zhaozhou had been there,
He would have carried out this imperative in reverse:
He'd have snatched the knife away,
And Nanquan would be begging for his life.

Case 15. Dongshan's Thirty Blows

When Dongshan came to study with Yunmen, Yunmen asked him, "Where have you just come from?" Dongshan said, "Chadu." Yunmen asked, "Where did you spend the summer?" Dongshan said, "At Baoci Temple in Hunan." Yunmen asked, "When did you leave there?" Dongshan said, "The twenty-fifth day of the eighth month." Yunmen said, "I forgive you thirty blows."

The next day Dongshan went back to ask about this. "Yesterday you forgave me thirty blows, but I do not know where I was at fault."

Yunmen said, "You rice-bag! [You've been through] Jiangxi and Hunan and you go on like this!"

At this Dongshan was greatly enlightened.

Wumen said,

At that moment, Yunmen immediately gave Dongshan the fundamental provisions and enabled him to come to life on another road. Yunmen would not let the Zen house be vacant. 295a

Dongshan spent a night in the sea of affirmation and denial. When morning came, he went again to Yunmen, who again explained it to him thoroughly. Then and there Dongshan was directly enlightened, and he was not impetuous by nature.

So I ask all of you, did Dongshan deserve the thirty blows or not? If you say he did, then all the grasses and trees and thickets and forests deserve thirty blows. If you say that Dongshan did not deserve thirty blows, then Yunmen becomes a liar. Only if you can understand clearly here can you share the same breath as Dongshan.

Verse

The lion teaches its cub a riddle.
[The cub] tries to leap forward, but already it's fallen.
For no reason, [the lion] tells it again
 and scores a direct hit.
The first arrow was superficial, the second struck deep.

Case 16. The Sound of the Bell, the Monk's Robe

Yunmen said, "The earth is so broad and wide—why do we put on the monk's robe at the sound of the bell?"

Wumen said,

All who learn Zen and study the Path must avoid following sounds and pursuing forms. Even if you awaken to the Path by hearing sound and illuminate the mind from seeing form, you are still an ordinary person. Little do you know that patch-robed monks ride on sound and get on top of form with wondrous illumination everywhere in everything.

But even so, tell me, does the sound come to the ear, or does the ear reach out to the sound? Even if sound and silence are both forgotten, when you reach this point, how can you understand in words? If you use the ears to hear, it is sure to be hard to understand. Only if you sense sounds with the eye will you be on intimate terms with Reality.

Verse

[For a worldly person,]
If you understand, everything is in the same family;
If you do not understand, thousands of differences and distinctions.
[For an enlightened person,]
If you do not understand, everything is in the same family;
If you do understand, thousands of differences and distinctions.

Case 17. The National Teacher Calls Three Times

The National Teacher called his attendant three times, and each time the attendant responded.

The National Teacher said, "I thought I was turning my back on you, but actually you were the one turning your back on me."

Wumen said,

When the National Teacher called three times, his tongue fell to the ground. The attendant's three responses were uttered in harmony with the light. The National Teacher was old and aloof; he pressed the ox's head down to make it eat the grass. But the attendant would not accept it; delicious food does not suit a man who is sated.

But tell me, where did he turn his back on him? When the public order is pure, talented children are valued. When the family is rich, the youngsters are spoiled.

Verse 295b

He makes people wear iron fetters with no openings,
Incriminating his descendants so none can be at ease.
If they want to prop open the door [to freedom],
They still must climb barefoot up the mountain of blades.

Case 18. Dongshan's Three Pounds of Hemp

When a monk asked Dongshan, "What is the Buddha?" Dongshan said, "Three pounds of hemp."

Wumen said,

Old man Dongshan had learned a bit of oyster Zen: as soon as he opens his shell, he shows his guts. Nevertheless, tell me, where will you see Dongshan?

Verse

Abruptly uttered: "Three pounds of hemp."
The words are close [to truth] and the intent even closer.
Those who come to talk of affirmation and denial
Are just affirmation-and-denial people.

Case 19. The Ordinary Mind Is the Path

When Zhaozhou asked Nanquan, "What is the Path?" Nanquan said, "The ordinary mind is the Path."

Zhaozhou said, "Can we go toward it or not?" Nanquan said, "As soon as you go toward it, you go against it."

Zhaozhou said, "If we do not try, how do we know it is the Path?" Nanquan said, "The Path is not in the province of knowing or not knowing. Knowing is false awareness. Not knowing is oblivion. If you really arrive on the Path of no trying, it is like space, empty all the way through. How can we impose affirmation and denial?"

At these words, Zhaozhou was suddenly enlightened.

Wumen said,

When Nanquan was questioned by Zhaozhou, he [disintegrated] like tiles scattering and ice melting and could not explain. But even if Zhaozhou did awaken, he still had to study thirty more years.

Verse

Spring has a hundred flowers . . . autumn has the moon.
Summer has cool winds . . . winter has the snow.
If there are no trivial things you hang your mind up on,
This is the good season in the human realm.

Case 20. The Person of Great Power

Master Songyuan said, "Why can't the person of great power take a step?" He also said, "Speaking the truth is not a mechanical act."

Wumen said,

It could be said that Songyuan spilled his guts, but there was no one to take up [the challenge he posed].

Even if you take it up, you should come to my place for
295c a sound beating. Why so? "If you want to know true gold,
observe it in fire."

Verse

He lifts his foot and kicks over the fragrant ocean.
Bowing his head, he looks down upon the four heavens of

meditative concentration.
One whole body . . . no place to put it.
Please fill in the line yourself.

Case 21. Yunmen's Piece of Shit

When a monk asked Yunmen, "What is the Buddha?" Yunmen said, "A dry piece of shit."

Wumen said,

What can be said about Yunmen? When the family is poor, even a simple meal is hard to manage. When things are busy, there is no time for even a hastily written letter. When he moves, he takes the piece of shit and props open the door with it, so that the rise and fall of the Buddhist Teaching can be seen.

Verse

Like a flash of lightning,
Or sparks struck from stone,
In the blink of an eye,
It's already gone.

Case 22. Kāśyapa's Temple Flagpole

Ānanda asked Kāśyapa, "Besides the golden robe [emblematic of successorship], what did the Buddha pass on to you?"

Kāśyapa called to him, "Ānanda!" Ānanda answered, "Yes?" Kāśyapa said, "Take down the temple flagpole in front of the gate [you are ready to take my place]."

Wumen said,

If you can utter a turning word here, you see in person the assembly on Spirit Peak in full array, still in session.

Otherwise, though Vipaśyin [earliest in the line of ancient Buddhas] already gave a care for you, up till now you still have not found the subtle wonder [of the Buddhas' message].

Verse

The question is not as intimate as the answer.
How many people will develop the means to see truth from this?
Elder brother calls, younger brother responds—exposing the family's ugliness.
This is a separate spring, that does not belong to [the cycles of natural polarities] *yin* and *yang*.

Case 23. Without Thinking of Good or Evil

[Intending to seize the robe and bowl emblematic of the Zen succession from Huineng, whom he regarded as a usurper] the monk Ming [a former military man] pursued the Sixth Patriarch Huineng [as he headed south from the Fifth Patriarch's place Huangmei in central China]. He overtook him in the Dayu Range [on the way to Guangdong].

When the Sixth Patriarch saw Ming coming, he threw the robe and bowl down on a rock and said, "This robe represents faith. Can it be taken away by force? I'll let you take it."

Ming went to pick it up, but it was as immovable as a mountain. Ming was alarmed and hesitated. He said, "I have come to seek the Dharma, not the robe and bowl. Please instruct me, workman." [Huineng had been a lowly workman at the Fifth Patriarch's place.]

The Sixth Patriarch said, "Without thinking of good, without thinking of evil, at just such a time, what is your original face?"

At this, Ming was greatly enlightened. His whole body was dripping with sweat. In tears, he bowed and asked, "Do you have any other intimate message beyond the intimate words and intimate meaning you have just communicated?"

The Sixth Patriarch said, "What I just told you is not intimate. 296a
If you reflect back on the face of your true self, what's intimate is within you."

Ming said, "Though I followed along with the congregation at the Fifth Patriarch's place, I never really had insight into the face of the true self. Today I have met with your instructions and gained entry. I am like a person drinking water who knows for himself whether it is cold or warm. Now you are my teacher, workman."

The Sixth Patriarch said, "If you are like this, then you and I both have the Fifth Patriarch as our teacher. Let us preserve [his teaching] well."

Wumen said,

> Regarding the Sixth Patriarch, one can say that this deed came from a house in a state of emergency. In his grandmotherly kindness, it was as if he peeled a fresh lichee, removed the pit, and put it in your mouth. All you have to do is swallow it.

Verse

> It cannot be described, it cannot be pictured,
> It cannot be praised enough—stop trying to sense it.
> There is no place to hide the original face;
> When the world crumbles, it does not decay.

Case 24. Apart from Words and Speech

A monk asked Master Fengxue, "Both speech and silence are involved with transcendent detachment and subtle wisdom. How can we pass through without error?"

Fengxue said, "I always remember Jiangnan in May; where the partridges call, the hundred flowers are fragrant."

Wumen said,

Fengxue's potential is like a flash of lightning: he finds a road and goes. But what can he do?—he cannot cut off the tongues of those who went before him.

If you can see on an intimate level here, then you naturally have a road on which to appear in the world.

As for the *samādhi* that is apart from words and speech, why don't you say something about it?

Verse

It is not revealed, the prime quality phrase;
Before it is spoken, it is already imparted.
When you step forward babbling,
We know you are totally at a loss for how to act.

Case 25. The Third-Ranked Monk Preaches the Dharma

Master Yangshan dreamed that he was at Maitreya's place as the third-ranked monk. One of the venerable ones there beat the gavel and announced, "Today the third-ranked monk will preach the Dharma."

[In his dream] Yangshan then got up, beat the gavel, and said, "The Mahayana Dharma is apart from all the permutations of propositional logic. Listen carefully, listen carefully!"

Wumen said,

Tell me, did he preach the Dharma or not? If he opens his mouth, he fails. If he keeps his mouth shut, he has also lost. Not opening, not shutting—one hundred eight thousand [possibilities].

Verse

White sun, blue sky,
Speaking of a dream in a dream,

Concocting strange apparitions,
Deceiving the whole congregation.

Case 26. Two Monks Roll Up a Curtain

Once the great Fayan of Qingliang was with some monks in front 296b
of his studio. When Fayan pointed to a curtain, two of the monks went to roll it up.

Fayan said, "One gains, one loses."

Wumen said,

Tell me, who gained and who lost? If you can focus the eye of enlightenment on this, you will know where Fayan met defeat. Nevertheless, you must not assess this in terms of gain and loss.

Verse

Roll it up: the illuminating light permeates space;
Even empty space does not suit our Zen school.
Far better, from emptiness, to abandon everything
For a close continuity that does not let the wind through.

Case 27. Not the Mind, Not the Buddha, Not Things

A monk asked Master Nanquan, "Is there a truth that has not been told to people?"

Nanquan said, "There is."

The monk asked, "What is the truth that has not been told to people?"

Nanquan said, "It is not the mind, not the Buddha, not things."

Wumen said,

When Nanquan was hit with this question, he totally hid away the family secret, acting rather shabby and decrepit.

Verse

Repeated admonitions would detract from your virtue;
Wordlessness is what is really effective.
Even if the blue sea itself were to change,
It still would never convey the message to you.

Case 28. Long Have We Heard of Longtan

Once when Deshan was getting instruction from Longtan, he stayed on into the night. Longtan said, "It's late—why don't you go?" Deshan said goodbye and lifted up the curtain [to go]. He saw it was dark out, so he turned back [to Longtan] and said, "It's dark outside."

Longtan then lit a candle and handed it to Deshan. As Deshan was about to take it, Longtan blew the candle out. At this Deshan suddenly had an insight. Then he bowed to Longtan. Longtan said, "What truth have you seen?" Deshan said, "From this day forward I shall no longer doubt the tongues of all the world's enlightened teachers."

The next morning Longtan went up to the teaching hall and said, "There's a guy here with teeth like a forest of swords and a mouth like a bowl of blood. Hit him a blow and he doesn't turn back. Someday in the future he will go to the summit of a solitary peak and establish our Path there."

Deshan then took all the commentaries he had written and brought them, along with a torch, to the area in front of the teaching hall. He held up the commentaries and said, "To plumb the depths of all the abstruse mystic theories is like placing a single hair in the void of space. To investigate to the end the workings of the world is like throwing a drop of water into a great abyss." Then he took his commentaries and burned them. After that he
296c paid homage to Longtan and said farewell.

Wumen said,

Before Deshan left [his home area in] Guangzhong [in northwest China], his heart was burning with zeal and his mouth was full of things to say. He travelled south intending to wipe out the [Zen] message of a special transmission outside the scriptural teachings.

When he reached Lizhou, he asked an old woman selling refreshments by the road if he could buy some. The old woman asked him, "What are those writings you have in your cart, Virtuous One?" Deshan said, "This is a commentary on the *Diamond Sutra*." The old woman said, "As it says in the Sutra, the past mind cannot be found, the present mind cannot be found, and the future mind cannot be found. Which mind do you wish to refresh, Virtuous One?"

When Deshan heard this question, his mouth sagged down into a frown. Nevertheless, he was still unwilling to die under the [impact of the] old woman's words. So he went on to ask the old woman, "Are there any Zen teachers around here?" The old woman said, "A couple of miles from here there is Master Longtan."

When Deshan got to Longtan, he incurred total defeat. We could say that his previous statements did not match his later words. Longtan acted as if unaware of the ugliness of a beloved child. When Longtan saw that Deshan had a bit of the spark [of arrogance] within him, he doused him over the head with some dirty water, totally drowning it out. If we look at their interaction with cold indifference, it was a good laugh.

Verse

[When seeking out an enlightened teacher,]
Hearing the name is not as good as seeing the face.
[From the viewpoint of the false expectations of the
teacher that the student brings,]
Seeing the face does not match hearing of the repute.
Though [Longtan] could save [Deshan's] nostrils,
What could he do?—he blinded his eyes.

Case 29. Not the Wind, Not the Flag

Once at the Sixth Patriarch's place, the wind was blowing and the [temple] flag was moving.

There were two monks arguing over this. One said it was the flag that was moving. One said it was the wind that was moving. They argued back and forth without reaching the truth.

The Sixth Patriarch told them, "It is not the flag moving, and it is not the wind moving; rather it is your minds that are moving." The two monks were startled.

Wumen said,

It is not the flag moving. It is not the wind moving. It is not the mind moving. Where will you see the Sixth Patriarch?

If you see intimately here, then you realize that the two monks were in the market for iron, but got gold. The Sixth Patriarch could not keep from laughing at this scene of indulgence.

Verse

Wind, flag, and mind moving—
The crimes are included in a single indictment.
They just knew how to open their mouths;
They were not aware their words fell.

Case 30. The Mind is the Buddha

When Damei asked, "What is the Buddha?" Mazu said, "The mind itself is the Buddha."

Wumen said,

If you can comprehend the total picture directly, then you
297a are wearing a Buddha's clothes, eating a Buddha's food, speaking a Buddha's words, and carrying out a Buddha's practice. Then you *are* a Buddha.

Even though this is the way it is, Damei has led a lot of people into accepting the calibrations on the balance beam [as a fixed standard]. Little do they know that anyone who says the word "Buddha" should wash out his or her mouth for three days.

If you are a person [in touch with your real identity], when you hear it said that the mind is the Buddha, you cover your ears and run out!

Verse

Blue sky, white sun—Don't seek!
If you're still asking what it's like,
You are crying out that you've been robbed,
But you have the loot in your hands.

Case 31. Zhaozhou Tests the Old Woman

[In the vicinity of Zhaozhou's place] a monk asked an old woman [whom he met along the road], "Which way is the road to Mount Taishan?" The old woman said, "Straight ahead." As soon as the monk walked on a few steps, the old woman said, "Such a fine monk, and still you go on like this?"

Later the monk brought this up to Zhaozhou. Zhaozhou said, "Wait until I go and check this old woman out for you." The next day Zhaozhou went [to where he could meet the old woman] and asked the same question as the monk. The old woman answered as she had before.

When Zhaozhou returned [to the monastery] he said to the assembly, "I have exposed the old woman of Taishan for you."

Wumen said,

The old woman only knew how to sit within her headquarters tent and launch her strategem to catch thieves [self-absorbed, self-styled "seekers"]. She did not know that old man Zhaozhou was good at using devices to steal into forts and seize defended strongpoints, and that he did not have the [outward] marks of a great man.

When we check them out, both [Zhaozhou and the old woman] had faults. But tell me, where did Zhaozhou expose the old woman?

Verse

The questions were the same,
And so were the answers.
In the cooked rice there is sand;
In the mud there are thorns.

Case 32. An Outsider Questions the Buddha

An outsider [a non-Buddhist] asked the World Honored One [the Buddha], "I do not ask about the verbal, and I do not ask about the nonverbal."

The World Honored One sat in his seat.

The outsider exclaimed in praise, "The great merciful compassion of the World Honored One has opened up the clouds of delusion for me and enabled me to enter [the truth]." Then he bowed in homage with full ceremony and left.

Later Ānanda asked the Buddha, "What realization did the outsider have that he went away praising you?"

The World Honored One said, "Like a good horse, he moved when he saw the shadow of the whip."

Wumen said,

Ānanda was the Buddha's disciple, yet he did not match the outsider in understanding. Tell me, how far apart are outsiders and the Buddha's disciples?

Verse

Walking on a sword's edge, 297b
Running up a hill of ice,
Not touching steps or a ladder,
Hanging from a cliff, let go.

Case 33. Not the Mind, Not the Buddha

Once when a monk asked, "What is the Buddha?" Mazu said, "Not the mind, not the Buddha."

Wumen said,

If you can see into this, your task of learning is complete.

Verse

When you meet a swordsman on the road, show him [your sword].
If you do not meet a poet, do not display [your verses].
If you meet someone [with potential], tell three-fourths [of the truth];
You should not give the whole of it.

Case 34. Wisdom Is Not the Path

Nanquan said, "The mind is not the Buddha. Wisdom is not the Path."

Wumen said,

We could say that Nanquan, though an old man, had no sense of shame. As soon as he opened his stinking mouth, he exposed his family's ugliness to the outside world. Even so, few appreciate his benevolence.

Verse

The sky clears, the sun comes out;
The rain falls, the ground is wet.
He fully explained the whole situation,
But I'm afraid you won't be able to believe him fully.

Case 35. When a Beautiful Woman's Spirit Departs

Wuzu asked a monk [at a funeral], "This beautiful woman has died and her spirit has departed. Which is the real person?"

Wumen said,

If you can awaken to the real person here, then you realize that both leaving and entering the shell [of worldly existence] is like sojourning in a travellers' inn.

If you cannot awaken to the real person here, don't go running around in confusion. When the physical elements that comprise your body suddenly disperse, you will be flailing around miserably like a crab dropped into boiling water. When that time comes, don't say I didn't tell you.

Verse

Clouds and moon are the same,
Streams and mountains all differ.
Myriad blessings, myriad blessings!
Are [we and they] one or two?

Case 36. If You Meet a Person Who Has Consummated the Path

Wuzu said, "If on the road you meet someone who has consummated the Path, don't use words or silence to reply. Tell me, how will you reply?"

Wumen said,

If you can reply on an intimate level here, how joyous! If not, you still must look everywhere.

Verse 297c

If on the road you meet a person who has consummated
the Path,
Don't use words or silence to reply.
A pinch on the cheek, a punch in the face,
If you understand directly then you understand.

Case 37. The Cypress in the Garden

[In nature the cypress is an evergreen tree, tall, straight, fragrant, and long-lived.] Once when a monk asked Zhaozhou, "What is the meaning of the Patriarch coming from the West?" Zhaozhou said, "The cypress tree in the garden."

Wumen said,

If you can see intimately into Zhaozhou's answer, then there's no Śākyamuni before and no Maitreya after.

Verse

Words cannot relate this matter [of enlightenment];
Speech cannot bring about the meeting of potentials.
Those who accept and serve words perish;
Those stuck on phrases are lost in delusion.

Case 38. A Water Buffalo Passing through a Window Frame

Wuzu said, "It's like a water buffalo passing through a window frame. Its horns and hooves have all passed through. Why can't the tail pass through?"

Wumen said,

If you can turn upside down here, focus the enlightened eye, and utter a turning word, then you will be able to repay the benevolence of all those who have protected and nurtured you and offer sustenance to [those in] the three realms [of desire, form, and the formless]. If not, you still have to pay attention to the tail to succeed.

Verse

If it passes through, it falls into a pit.
If it turns back, it is still ruined.
This bit of tail
Is indeed very strange.

Case 39. Yunmen's "You Have Said Something Improper"

As a monk was questioning Yunmen, "The light shines quiescent throughout countless worlds. The one phrase is not cut off... ", Yunmen interrupted, "Aren't these the words of the distinguished literatus [of the Tang period, an adept in Buddhism] Zhang Zhuo?"

The monk admitted, "They are."

Yunmen said, "You have said something improper."

Later Sixin cited this and said, "Tell me, where did the monk say something improper?"

Wumen said,

If in this case you can see that Yunmen's functioning was solitary and dangerous, and why the monk said something improper, then you are fit to be a teacher of humans and devas. If you are not yet clear about these points, then you cannot even save yourself.

Verse

A hook hangs down in a swift flowing stream;
Those who crave the bait are caught.
As soon as they open their mouths a crack,
Their lives and true identities are lost. 298a

Case 40. Kicking Over the Water Jar

When Master Weishan was still in Baizhang's congregation, he served as an administrator. Baizhang was about to select someone to be the master on Mount Dawei. He invited Weishan and the head monk forward in front of the assembly and said, "The one who goes beyond patterns can go [be the Zen master on Mount Dawei]."

Baizhang then took out a water jar and set it on the ground, posing the question, "If you could not call it a water jar, what would you call it?"

The head monk said, "It cannot be called a tree trunk."

Then Baizhang asked Weishan. Weishan kicked over the water jar and left.

Baizhang laughed and said, "The head monk has lost the mountain." Then he dispatched Weishan to open [the center at] Dawei.

Wumen said,

Weishan was one of the bravest people of his time, but even he could not jump clear of Baizhang's trap. When we check this case out, Weishan should have taken things more seriously, rather than make light of it. Why? Away with evil spirits! He managed to take off his cloth head-wrap, but he loaded an iron cangue onto his shoulders.

Verse

Tossing off the water scoop and the dipper,
A direct burst cuts off all roundabout measures.

Baizhang's double barrier cannot hold him back;
The point of his foot leaps over countless Buddhas.

Case 41. Bodhidharma Pacifies the Mind

Bodhidharma sat facing a wall. Huike [who would be his successor] stood in the snow and cut off his arm, saying, "My mind is not at peace. Please, Teacher, pacify my mind."

Bodhidharma said, "Bring out your mind and I will pacify it for you."

Huike said, "When I search for my mind, ultimately it cannot be found."

Bodhidharma said, "I have already pacified your mind for you."

Wumen said,

The gap-toothed old barbarian sailed thousands of miles to come to China on a special mission. This could be called "raising waves where there is no wind." At last he accepted a single disciple, but even he was missing an arm.

Alas for the people in ordinary worldly life who are illiterate [towards the mystic tradition]!

Verse

Bodhidharma came from the West, directly pointing [to the inherent real mind];
This business [Zen] arose from what he imparted.
He grated on the ears of the [would-be] Buddhist community,
[Telling them] "It's been you all along."

Case 42. The Girl Comes Out of Samādhi

In ancient times Mañjuśrī [the great Bodhisattva who represents transcendent wisdom] was present where all the enlightened ones were assembled with the World Honored One. When the time came that all the enlightened ones were returning to their own countries, there was a girl [left behind] sitting in *samādhi* near the Buddha.

Mañjuśrī then asked the Buddha, "How is it that a girl may sit so close to the Buddha but I may not?"

The Buddha told Mañjuśrī, "Just arouse this girl from her *samādhi* and ask her yourself."

Mañjuśrī circled three times round the girl and snapped his 298b
fingers; then he took her into all the heavens of sublime form and of meditative bliss. Mañjuśrī used up all his spiritual powers without being able to bring her out of *samādhi*.

The World Honored One said, "Even hundreds of thousands of Mañjuśrīs could not bring this girl out of her *samādhi*. But if you go down past twelve hundred million worlds, there is a Bodhisattva [called] Ignorance who can bring this girl out of *samādhi*."

At that instant the Mahāsattva Ignorance welled up from the ground and bowed in homage to the World Honored One. The World Honored One directed Ignorance [to arouse the girl from *samādhi*], so he went over to the girl and snapped his fingers once. At this the girl came out of *samādhi*.

Wumen said,

When old man Śākyamuni staged this play, it was not to convey something trivial. But tell me, Mañjuśrī was the teacher of seven Buddhas; why couldn't he bring the girl out of *samādhi*? Ignorance was only a Bodhisattva in the first stage [which is joy brought on by faith in the Dharma]; why then could he bring her out of it? If you can see on an intimate level here, then the frantic haste of karmic consciousness is the great *samādhi* of the dragon kings, the Nāgas, the keepers of wisdom.

Verse

Whether [Mañjuśrī] can bring you out or not,
She and you are on your own.

Spirit heads and demon faces
Meet defeat in the flowing wind.

Case 43. Shoushan's Bamboo Comb

Master Shoushan held up a bamboo comb and showed it to the assembly saying, "If you call it a comb, you trespass on it. If you do not call it a comb, you turn your back on it. Tell me, all of you, what will you call it?"

Wumen said,

If you call it a comb, you trespass on it. If you do not call it a comb, you turn your back on it. You cannot say anything, and you cannot say nothing. Quickly, speak!

Verse

Holding up a bamboo comb,
Carrying out the imperative to kill and bring to life,
Turning away and trespassing gallop together,
Buddhas and Patriarchs beg for their lives.

Case 44. Bajiao's Staff

Master Bajiao taught the assembly, "If you have a staff, I will give you a staff. If you have no staff, I will take your staff away."

Wumen said,

It supports you as you cross Broken Bridge River and accompanies you as you return to No-Moon Village. If you call it a staff, you enter hell like a shot.

Verse

Everyone everywhere, deep and shallow—
They are all within his grip.

He props up heaven and supports the earth, 298c
Energizing the wind of Zen [its transformative influence]
wherever he is.

Case 45. Who Is *He*?

Master Yan of East Mountain said, "Even Śākyamuni and Maitreya are *his* slaves. Tell me, who is *he*?

Wumen said,

If you see *him* clearly, it is like meeting your father at a crossroads; you don't have to ask anyone else if it's him or not.

Verse

Don't grasp anyone else's bow [but *his*; *he* is the real you];
Don't ride anyone else's horse;
Don't commit anyone else's misdeeds;
Don't mind anyone else's business.

Case 46. Step Forward from the Top of the Pole

Master Shishuang said, "At the top of the hundred foot pole, how will you take a step forward?"

Another ancient worthy said, "Though the person sitting on top of the hundred foot pole has found entry, it is still not real. At the top of the hundred foot pole you must step forward and make manifest the complete body [of Reality] throughout the worlds of the ten directions."

Wumen said,

If you can advance a step and transform your being, then there is no place to shun because you cannot act enlightened there.

But tell me, how do you step forward from the top of a hundred foot pole? With an exclamation of surprise?

Verse

Blinding the eye of enlightenment,
Wrongly accepting [as absolute] the calibrations on the scale,
Staking their bodies and lives and throwing them away,
One blind person leading a blind crowd.

Case 47. Tuṣita's Three Barriers

Master Yue of Tuṣita Temple posed three barriers to question students: "You push aside the crude superficialities, the weeds, to study the hidden truth, in order to see your real nature. But right now where *is* your real nature?

"Only after you recognize your real nature do you escape from birth and death. But when your eyesight fails [with physical death], how *do* you escape?

"When you have escaped from birth and death, you know where you are going. When the physical elements [that comprise your body] disperse, where *will* you go?"

Wumen said,

If you can use these three turning words, then you can act the master wherever you go and merge with the source [of Reality] while encountering causal circumstances.

Otherwise, it is easy to fill up on coarse food; chew it fine and it is hard to go hungry.

Verse

In a single moment of mind, observing from a universal viewpoint countless eons,
The task of these infinite eons is right now.
Right now see through this one moment,
See through the person now observing.

Case 48. Qianfeng's One Road

A monk asked Qianfeng, “All those blessed with excellent enlight- 299a
enment in all worlds share one road to nirvana. Where does the road start?”

Qianfeng picked up his staff and drew a line and said, “Right here.”

Later a monk asked Yunmen for instruction. Yunmen picked up a fan and said, “The fan leaps up to the thirty-third heaven and taps Indra on the nose. In the Eastern Sea it strikes a carp and the rain pours down.”

Wumen said,

> One man walks on the bottom of the deepest sea, raising dust and dirt as though winnowing. One man stands on the peak of the highest mountain, with white waves surging up to the sky. Holding fast, letting go, each extends one hand to support the Zen vehicle. They are like two galloping chargers colliding; surely no one in the world can stand up to them. But if we observe them with the correct eye, neither of the two great elders knows where the road starts.

Verse

> Before you've set out, you've already arrived.
> Before you've spoken, you've already explained.
> Even if you anticipate every situation before it develops,
> You still have to know that there is an opening upwards.

Afterword by Wumen

When the Buddhas and enlightened teachers since antiquity imparted enlightenment stories, they settled cases on the basis of the facts. There was never any excess of words.

They lift off your brain cover and display the eye of enlightenment. They want everyone to take it up directly, not to seek elsewhere. If you are a person of integrity who can comprehend such methods, as soon as you hear them mentioned, you know where they're at.

Ultimately there is no gateway that can be entered, nor any steps that can be climbed. You must throw back your shoulders and cross through the barrier without asking the border guard.

Haven't you seen what Xuansha said? "The gate of nothingness, the gate of No, is the gate of liberation. Mindfulness of No, the absence of deluded ideation, is the mindfulness of people of the Path."

Moreover, Baiyun said, "You must clearly realize: it's just this. Why can't you pass through?" Even this kind of talk is rubbing red clay on a cow's udder [dirtying a source of pure nourishment].

If you can manage to pass through the barrier of the gate of No, you have already made a fool out of me. If you cannot pass through the barrier of the gate of No, you have turned your back on your true self.

As it is said, the mind of nirvana is easy to have insight into, but differentiating wisdom is hard to clarify. If you can be clear in differentiating wisdom, the family and the nation will spontaneously be at peace.

Dated the first year of the Shao Ding era [1228], five days before the end of the summer retreat. By the monk Huikai of Wumen, eighth-generation descendant of Yangqi.

Addenda

Zen Prescriptions

Following guidelines and keeping to rules is binding yourself without rope. Being unobstructed in all directions is an army of de-
299b luded demons. Keeping the mind clear and still is the perverted Zen of silent illumination.

Indulging your inclinations oblivious of entanglements is falling into a deep pit. Being alert and awake and undimmed is wearing chains and a cangue. Thoughts of good, thoughts of evil are hell and heaven. Opinions on the Buddha and the Dharma are twin iron mountains encircling you. If you awaken just as thought arises, you are someone playing with the spirit. If you sit inert cultivating concentration, this is a plan for living in the ghosts' house. If you advance, you are missing the truth; if you retreat, you go against the Zen school. If you neither advance nor retreat, you have the breath of life but are dead.

So tell me, how should you act? If you make the effort, you must finish in this life. Don't go on forever suffering more disasters.

Huanglong's Three Barriers by Zongshou

How is my hand like a Buddha's hand?
Reaching behind me for the pillow,
Unknowingly I laugh aloud.
Actually the whole body is a hand.

How is my foot like a donkey's foot?
Before I set out, it has already taken a step.
I let it wander sideways across the whole world,
Walking three-footed upside-down over [our Zen ancestor]
  Yanqi.

Every person has a causal nexus in life;
Every person can penetrate through to before this
  mechanism operates.
[The fearsome monster Eight-Armed] Nāṭa breaks bones to
  take back to his father.
How could [a real Zen adept like] the Fifth Patriarch depend
On his karmic links with his papa [the Fourth Patriarch]?

Buddha's hand, a donkey's foot, the causal nexus of life—
Not the Buddha, not the Path, not Zen.

Don't be surprised that Wumen's barrier is dangerous.
It is the total enemy of patch-robed ones.

In recent days at Ruiyan we have Wumen;
He stays on the meditation bench and judges ancient and
modern.
The roads of ordinary and holy are both cut off;
So many worms hidden in the earth begin to speak with
the voice of thunder.

Let the head monk of Wumen and the monks assembled here now join to offer a mountain verse in thanks.

[Dated and signed] Shao Ding era, geng-yin in the cycle of years [A.D. 1230], late spring. Written by Zongshou of Wuliang.

Afterword by Meng Hong to the 1245 Reprinting

Bodhidharma came from the West. He did not cling to words; he directly indicated the human mind, so people could see their real nature and become enlightened.

To say "directly indicated" is already roundabout. To say further "become enlightened" is rather embarrassing. Since there is no gate to Wumen's No-gate, the gate of nothingness, why is there a barrier? The evil sound of his grandmotherly concern has spread. I want to add an extra word to make forty-nine cases. The few places here that are hard to understand should be comprehended in a lift of the eyebrows.

Reprinted in the summer of the *yi-si* year of the Chun You era [A.D. 1245]. Afterword by Meng Hong, Military Inspector, Military Governor of the Baoning Army Region, Pacification and Settlement High Commissioner for the Jing-Hu Region and concurrently Garrison-Colony Commissioner and Grand Policy Response Commissioner for Kui Circuit and Superintendent of Jiangling-fu and

Handong-jun, Lord Founder of the State, enfeoffed with the revenue of 2,100 households, with a hundred families in direct domain.

Case 49

[By the layman Anwan, Zheng Qingzhi (d. 1251), official, scholar, and Zen student.]

Old Zen man Wumen made forty-eight cases, passing judgments on 299c
the public cases of the ancient worthies. He is just like a seller of fried cakes. As soon as the buyer opens his mouth and takes one, Wumen makes it so that he can neither swallow it nor spit it out.

Nevertheless, I want to put another one on his hot griddle, so we have enough for extra. But if it's offered up as before, I wonder where you old teachers will sink your teeth? If you can eat it up in one mouthful, then you emit light and move the earth. If not, then you will see the forty-eight [fried cakes] all turn into hot sand. Speak quickly! Speak quickly!

[Case:] In the *[Lotus] Sutra* [the Buddha] says, "Stop! Stop! You must not speak. My Dharma is wondrous and inconceivable."

Anwan says,

Where does the Dharma come from? From whence does the wonder exist? And what is it when [the Buddha] is preaching? Not only were [the eminent Zen teachers like] Fenggan talkative, but Śākyamuni actually had a lot to say too. The old ones concocted weird apparitions and have caused generations of their descendants to get tripped up by the further ramifications, the "creeping vines," so they cannot escape. Extraordinary word-handles like these cannot function as spoons or steamers. How many people have misunderstood!

A bystander asked, "Ultimately how will you wrap up the case and pass judgment?"

Anwan touched his ten fingertips together and said, "Stop! Stop! You must not speak. My Dharma is wondrous and inconceivable. Turn quickly to this word inconceivable." Then he drew a small circle [in the air], pointed to it, and said to the assembly, "The whole canon of verbal teachings, and Vimalakīrti's [wordless] Dharma-gate of nonduality, are all in here."

Verse

The fire of words is a lamp;
You turn your head but there's no answer.
Only a thief recognizes a thief;
With a single question it's inherited.

[Dated and signed] Chun You era, *bing-wu* year [1246], late summer. Written by the layman Anwan of Chuji at Fisherman's Farm on West Lake.

Colophon

Since the old printing blocks were destroyed, it was ordered that they be remade. When the work of carving them was completed, these printing blocks were placed in Guangyuan Zen Temple on Tuṣita Mountain in Wuzangzhou. Dated the thirteenth day of the tenth month of the *yi-jiu* year of the Ying Yong era. In the custody of the *bhikṣu* Ganyuan.

The Faith-Mind Maxim

Translated from the Chinese
Taishō Volume 48, Number 2010

by

YOSHIDA Osamu

Translator's Introduction

I. Author

The *Xin-xin-ming* is attributed to Seng-can. The *Xu-kao-seng-zhuan* (645–667 C.E.) mentions him as the successor to Hui-ke, the Second Patriarch in the Chinese Zen lineage without further specifics. The *Bao-lin-zhuan* (801) gives the date of his passing as 606 C.E. It tells us that his remains were found and part of them were sent to Shen-hui (746). A memorial tower was dedicated to him, and Emperor Xuan-zheng (or rather Dai-zheng) gave him the posthumous title of Jing-chi (Mirror-insight) (751). Usually he is called the Third Patriarch Seng-can or Jian-chi (Mirror-insight) Seng-can.

Passages from the *Xin-xin-ming* are quoted and ascribed to the Third Patriarch in the *Recorded Words* of Bai-cheng Huai-hai (749–814). Later on the work was quoted, giving it an authority equivalent to that of the scriptures, in the *Recorded Words* of various Buddhist teachers, including Zhao-zhou (778–897), Huang-bo (?–850), Lin-ji (?–866), and Tong-shan (807–867), and in other works.

The *Jing-de-zhuan-deng-lu* (1004) gives the following dialogue between Seng-can and the Second Patriarch, Hui-ke. (A similar conversation between the latter and the First Patriarch, Bodhidharma, is also reported.)

> Seng-can said, "I am bound up in sickness. Please purify my sins."
>
> Hui-ke said, "Bring your sins out. I shall purify them."
>
> Seng-can, after a long while, said, "I have sought them, but could not grasp my sins."
>
> Hui-ke said, "I have now purified your sins."

Under Hui-ke, Seng-can renounced secular life and was given Dharma transmission. He went to Mount Si-kun in Shu Province, where he encountered the persecution of Buddhists by Emperor Wu of the Northern Chu (574). He hid in the same province on Mount Wan-gong, where he met Dao-xin, who later became the Fourth Patriarch. Afterward he went to Mount Luo-fu. Seng-can reportedly passed away standing while holding out a branch to his assembly.

II. The *Xin-xin-ming*

A. Significance

Form. The *Xin-xin-ming* contains the profound and practical essence of Buddhism in a brief and beautiful form. Its verse style facilitates melodious chanting, is easy to memorize, and elucidates the tenets. In particular, the lines of four characters (syllables) make superb aphorisms. Thus, on any occasion, any verse or line could reveal profound meaning to the reader and effect an explosive experience.

The work is made up of thirty-six verses, totalling five hundred eighty-four characters. Each verse contains two rhymed sentences, each composed of two lines of four characters, each rhymed ABCB. Sometimes the first or third line shares the rhyme. Verse 30 has three sentences (six lines). The context, the rhyme, and variant texts suggest that one sentence is missing, or that some changes were made over time.

Content. The *Xin-xin-ming* encompasses the thought of Early Buddhism and later developments such as the Voidness School, the Representation-only School, and the Flower Garland School. It expressly extols the essence of the Mahayana (Great Vehicle) and, above all, the One Vehicle (unity of all) ideal. It clarifies unique Zen attitudes, such as not depending on words by being beyond all discriminations and conventions, directly pointing to the mind (i.e., the One Mind), seeing one's own nature by returning to the root, (right awakening for everyone), and becoming a Buddha.

Authorship. The *Xin-xin-ming* is neither a Sutra (a scripture claiming the Buddha's authorship, even if produced at a later time), nor a Shastra (elucidation of the Buddha's teaching by a scholar). It claims to be and is recognized as an independent work comparable to a Sutra by a Buddha (Awakened One). It is one of the first works with the unique understanding and attitude that every being has Buddha-nature and can become a Buddha.

Considered in light of these points, the *Xin-xin-ming* may be regarded as the first revolutionary work in the Zen tradition or in Chinese Buddhism. Earlier works, such as those ascribed to Bodhidharma in the Zen tradition or to Tien-tai Chi-i outside the Zen tradition, do not match this work in form and content, or in historical impact and popularity.

This work made it clear that anyone can become a Buddha, can ascertain what Buddhahood is, and can share Buddhahood with all, including insentient beings. This was revolutionary, for before Seng-can, traditional Buddhists gradually came to believe that attaining Buddhahood was more and more difficult, and required eons, so that it came to be regarded as impossible. This work opened the way for people to learn to become a Buddha themselves, rather than just learning what the Buddha taught.

This work also opened the way for other popular verse works, such as Yong-jia Xuan-jue's *Zheng-dao-ge (Song of Verifying the Way)*, Shi-tou Xi-qian's *San-dong-qi (Merging of Sameness and Difference)*, Tong-shan Liang-jia's *Bao-jing-san-mei (Jewel Mirror Samādhi)*, the *Han-shan-shi (Han-shan's Poems)*, and the *Recorded Words* of various authors. Thus it facilitated the blooming of Mahayana Buddhism in the general culture.

Its direct and practical significance, at a more personal level, lies in the way it presents the Buddha-dharma (awakened form). It answers the questions of how, why, where, and when.

It tells how to become a Buddha. If one avoids fabrications (discriminative thinking and actions), one can realize the true nature of existence. The concrete method is meditation [*dhyāna=jhān(a)=zen*], by which Gotama became a Buddha. In meditation, one stops all physical and mental fabrications and experiences total harmony (before discrimination), unconditioned peace (nirvana), and awakening *(bodhi)* to the Law (Dharma=norm) of Dependent Origination, which states that all phenomena (dharmas=forms) originate dependent upon causes and conditions (which means that they all are related and relative).

When one knows that this law operates universally throughout time and space, one knows that anyone and anything can fit into it, anywhere and at any time. This insight provides a true base and force for the Great Vehicle and the One Vehicle (which maintains that all have Buddha-nature and that all are one), and for the ideal of the Bodhisattva (awakening beings who vow to save all beings before saving themselves). The Great Vehicle ideal shifts the stress from freedom *from* body and mind to freedom (free use) *of* body and mind. Therefore, realizing the Buddha-nature in everyday actions (dharmas), here and now, becomes essential.

The Zen movement returns to the Buddha's core method of meditation and its application in everyday life, and to his Bodhisattva (Mahayana, One Vehicle) ideal and its application in the world. The *Xin-xin-ming* was the first treatise which declared and delineated this movement. It promises everyone a life of the Dharma (truthful, lawful), a genuine limitless life in true peace, and welfare together with all beings.

B. Title

Xin (faith) in Buddhism translates the Sanskrit *prasāda*. It means neither belief in a dogma nor belief in an ordinary mind, as it is often wrongfully interpreted. It means the stable, serene state in which within and without are one; a state realized in complete concentration *(samādhi)* and comprehension, in which all discriminations and doubts are cleared away (verse 28). "Faith" means to settle in absolute truth or ultimate reality (Dharma) itself. It is thoroughly clear (verse 1) and beyond speech, time, and space (verses 32–36).

Xin (mind) in the Zen tradition is not the mind located in the heart or in the brain, but the mind in any form such as a pebble, a pillar, the earth, or the entire universe. This is consistent with the Buddhist tradition that the mind is inseparable from dharmas (mental objects) (verse 14). Although *xin* (faith) and *xin* (mind) in the conventional sense are concerned respectively with object and subject, in ultimate reality they are not different (verse 36).

Ming (maxim) means engraving. It stands for the engraving of the truth (Dharma) on the mind, or the engraving of the true nature (Dharma) of the faith-mind so that it will never be forgotten. It is the experience and expression of the author and the expounding of the truth for all. To avoid conventional traps, we need to caution ourselves constantly to return to or remain in the ultimate truth. The *Xin-xin-ming* exists so that everyone can settle in the original, unfabricated faith-mind.

C. Content and Context

Owing to its verse form, its recurring ideas, and its not being a dissertation, it is difficult to determine the overall structure of this work. However, there is a general flow leading to the conclusion, and a succession of topics. It is clear that the rhyme scheme determines the verse units. Then from the content, two neighboring verses are usually paired (either in parallel or in contrast). Further, two neighboring pairs of verses are likely to be coupled. Furthermore, often these units are again coupled. This makes five divisions (or seven divisions if we consider the first two verses as the preface and the last two as the conclusion). The topics in parentheses are taken from the first verse of each pair of consecutive verses. The five divisions are:

1. Perfecting the Way (perfect Way/mind disease/balance in oneness/oneness);
2. Returning to the root (return to the root/unborn mind/one voidness/great Way);
3. Right awakening (no leaving-stopping/One Vehicle/right awakening/duality);
4. No duality (One Thusness/unfabricated/unretained/no duality);
5. Faith-mind (greatest is smallest/all is one).

1. Perfecting the Way lies in avoiding discrimination. Dichotomies such as love and hate or subject and object are the subjects of more than twenty of the thirty-six verses. Mental fabrication (discriminative thinking and attitude) is actually the first misstep in the (Awakened) Way, on which one sets out to find oneself (verses 1–4).

We must stop these relative views and attitudes and settle in the absolute One Dharma World of Thusness (reality) as if in cloudless, comprehensive, clear, and creviceless space (verses 5–8).

2. Returning to the root is to turn the light on oneself. The Awakened Way is realized by returning to the root source, reflecting on oneself, stopping all measuring thoughts *(fei-si-liang)*, i.e., profound meditation (verses 9–12). All dichotomies (subject and object, mind and matter, etc.) are dependent and relative, not absolute entities; they are interdependently originated from one voidness. (The entire world is interdependent.) Missing this is missing the right way (verses 13–16).

3. Right awakening is to realize the oneness of all dharmas. The law penetrating reality is universal and eternal; it neither leaves nor stops. Mental fabrications (discriminative intellect and emotion) becloud and darken the real state (Thusness) of phenomena (the Dharma world), and true freedom is lost (verses 17–24). Solid sitting clears away mental fabrications, just as water in a still bowl becomes clear. Turbulence and turbidity depart, and the real world is reflected clearly.

4. No duality is realized in the Dharma world of Thusness. Mental fabrications distort and reify dynamic reality and functions. In unmoved sitting, one settles in oneness and Thusness, and becomes totally clear and cleared (unconditioned). Awakening is a clearing away of the clouds so that one regains a total perspective, terminates all doubts and suffering, and establishes oneself in truth (Dharma=existential *forms* and the *norm* operating therein, i.e., the Law of Dependent Origination). Dependent Origination penetrates existence, which means that there is interrelation and relativity, unity and voidness (verses 25–32).

5. Faith is the mind settled in the Dharma world. A classic example of Dependent Origination is Indra's net, which has a crystal ball at each of its knots. Any one crystal ball reflects all the crystal balls, including itself, infinitely: thus all are in one and one is in all. Any single leaf or life is thus interpenetrated with the entire world. Nothing is separate. "No duality" is reality, the true mind, and the genuine faith. One Mind, one Thusness (the Dharma world), one voidness, and faith are the same reality of oneness realized in deep

samādhi as expressed in *i-yuan-shan* (a state of perfect unity) (verses 33–36).

Reading Zen materials must be done not only with the mind, but with the body and world also. To attain the Way or achieve the Dharma means to embody the Dharma (norm=Dependent Origination; form=mind, mouth, body, water, wind, and world). It is to see no dharma separate from oneself, to know existence as voidness, to regard the smallest thing as the greatest matter, to experience an instant as a million years, and to roam free and live fully a million years here and now (in an instant).

III. Text and Translation

The text used is the one in the *Taishō Daizōkyō*, Vol. 48. The variant readings given in Taishō notes 7 and 8 were used.

This translation is intended to be as faithful as possible to the original in its content and style. Each verse line corresponds to one line of four characters in the original. Lines appear in the same sequence and are rhymed or related in the ending sounds. The second line of verse 32 ("A million years are a mind moment") was chosen over another version in the *Taishō*, because of the ending sound.

The Faith-Mind Maxim

The perfect Way is not difficult; 376b17
It only avoids discrimination.
If only there is no love or hate,
Completely clean and clear is it. (1)

If there's the slightest discrepancy,
There is the heaven-earth separation.
If you want to realize it presently,
There should be no liking or disliking. (2)

Conflict 'tween liking and disliking;
This is the disease of the mind.
Not knowing this profound tenet,
You toil to appease the mind in vain. (3)

It is perfect like vast space,
Neither deficient nor superfluous.
Due to attachments and aversions,
Indeed never realized is Thusness. (4)

Follow not the existential condition;
Dwell not in the voidness-conception.
Settle in stable balance in oneness;
All vanish by themselves in sereneness. (5)

Stopping motion to return to stillness
Keeps ever in motion that stillness.
Lingering solely in both extremes,
How can you ever realize oneness? (6)

Unless you penetrate oneness,
You cannot succeed in either way.
Neglecting existence, you lose it;
Following voidness, you violate it. (7)

The more speech and thought,
The more you become separated.
376c No more speech and thought,
Nowhere is ever unpenetrated. (8)

Returning to the root attains the tenet;
Following the illumination loses the source.
Reflecting the light back even an instant
Wins mastery over the confronting voidness. (9)

Transformations of the confronting voidness
All come forth from deluded views.
It's of no use trying to seek the truth;
You need only stop creating views. (10)

Never adhere to dualistic views,
And sincerely avoid pursuing them.
With even a hint of right and wrong,
The mind is lost in total confusion. (11)

Duality comes from the one,
But the one shouldn't be cherished.
If the one mind is not born,
Myriad dharmas do not offend. (12)

No offense, and no dharma,
No birth, and so no mind.
Subjects vanish following objects;
Objects disappear following subjects. (13)

Objects are objects due to subjects;
Subjects are subjects due to objects.
When you know these two intimately,
They are one voidness originally. (14)

One voidness is equal to both of these,
Equally encompassing all forms.
When you've no views of coarse and subtle,
How can there be any partiality at all? (15)

The great Way's essence is vast,
And it's neither easy nor difficult.
The small view strays in doubts;
The hastier it is, the tardier it gets. (16)

Sticking to this view, you go beyond bounds,
And are sure to enter into wrong roads.
Giving up this view, you are in naturalness,
Where the true essence neither leaves nor stops. (17)

Trusting in nature, you fit into the Way,
Roaming free with disturbance out of the way.
Hanging onto thoughts separates you from truth;
Sinking into darkness is unsound in truth. (18)

Unsoundness troubles the spirit;
What use is it to be estranged or intimate?
If you wish to enter the One Vehicle,
Hate not the six-sense dust particle. (19)

By not hating the six-sense dust particle,
You are one with awakening in truth.
The wise make no fabrications themselves;
The ignorant make bonds for themselves. (20)

The Dharma has no dharmas separated;
You only are delusively attached.
The mind toils with the mind;
Isn't this a great error indeed? (21)

In delusion, rest and unrest are produced;
In awakening, like and dislike are cleared away.
All dualities are fabricated
By yourself, discriminating and deluded. (22)

Emptiness-flowers and dream-delusions,
Why these do you toil to grasp and embrace?
Throw away gain and loss,
Right and wrong, all at once. (23)

If the eyes do not sleep themselves,
All dreams cease of themselves.
If the mind makes no discriminations,
All dharmas remain in one Thusness. (24)

Profound in the reality of one Thusness,
You are unmoved and unconditioned.
All dharmas visioned in equality,
You return to true naturalness. (25)

Even its cause is untraceable,
And no comparison is available.
Motion ceasing, no motion is there;
Cessation moved, no cessation is there. (26)

When two are not achieved,
How could there be oneness?
When all is exhausted,
There remain no measures. (27)

When the mind settles in equanimity,
Fabrications come to rest.
Doubts are resolved in total clarity,
And right faith settles straight. (28)

When nothing is retained,
Nothing is to be remembered.
In self-illumination, vast and clear,
The mind's power exerts itself no more. (29)

Where there is no more measuring,
377a Intellect-emotion has no fathoming.

In the Dharma world of Thusness,
There is neither self nor others.
If you deem to fit into it at once,
"No duality" is the only utterance. (30)

In no duality, all in sameness,
Nothing remains unembraced.
The wise ones in the ten directions,
All enter into this great truth. (31)

Truth being beyond long and short,
A million years are a mind-moment.
Neither existent nor nonexistent,
The ten directions are right in front. (32)

The greatest being the smallest,
Reified realms are fully forgotten.
The smallest being the greatest,
Expressed ends are utterly unseen. (33)

Existence is itself voidness,
Voidness is itself existence.
If Thusness is not realized
Never tarry there indeed. (34)

One is all,
All is One.
If Thusness is ably realized,
Why worry you as unperfected? (35)

Nonduality is faith and mind,
No duality is the faith-mind.
Unreached by the path of words,
Unlimited by past, present, or future. (36)

Bibliography

R. H. Blyth. "The Hsinhsinming (The Believing Mind)." In *Zen and Zen Classics*. Vol. 1. Tokyo: Hokuseido, 1960.

Taisen Deshimaru. "Shin jin mei; poème Zen sur la foi en l'esprit de maître Sosan (?–606)." In *Textes sacrès du Zen (Ch'an)*. Vol. 2. Paris: Edition Seghers, 1976.

Philip Kapleau. "Affirming Faith in Mind." In *Zen: Dawn in the West*. New York: Anchor Press Doubleday, 1979.

Shuhei Ohasama. "Schindjin-mej (Stempel des Glaubens von dem dritten Patriarch Szōzan)." In *Zen: der lebendige Buddhismus in Japan*. Stuttgart: F. A. Perthes, 1925.

Richard Robinson. "Faith in Mind." In *Chinese Buddhist Verses*. London: John Murray, 1954.

D. T. Suzuki. "On Believing in Mind." In *Manual of Zen Buddhism*. Kyoto: Eastern Buddhist Society, 1935.

Arthur Waley. "On Trust in the Heart." In *Buddhist Texts through the Ages*. New York: Philosophical Library, 1954.

Index

A List of the Volumes of the BDK English Tripiṭaka

(First Series)

Abbreviations

Ch.: Chinese
Skt.: Sanskrit
Jp.: Japanese
Eng.: Published title
T.: Taishō Tripiṭaka

Vol. No.		Title	*T.* No.
1, 2	*Ch.*	Ch'ang-a-han-ching （長阿含經）	1
	Skt.	Dīrghāgama	
3–8	*Ch.*	Chung-a-han-ching （中阿含經）	26
	Skt.	Madhyamāgama	
9-I	*Ch.*	Ta-ch'eng-pên-shêng-hsin-ti-kuan-ching （大乘本生心地觀經）	159
9-II	*Ch.*	Fo-so-hsing-tsan （佛所行讃）	192
	Skt.	Buddhacarita	
10-I	*Ch.*	Tsa-pao-ts'ang-ching （雜寶藏經）	203
	Eng.	The Storehouse of Sundry Valuables	
10-II	*Ch.*	Fa-chü-p'i-yü-ching （法句譬喩經）	211
11-I	*Ch.*	Hsiao-p'in-pan-jo-po-lo-mi-ching （小品般若波羅蜜經）	227
	Skt.	Aṣṭasāhasrikā-prajñāpāramitā-sūtra	
11-II	*Ch.*	Chin-kang-pan-jo-po-lo-mi-ching （金剛般若波羅蜜經）	235
	Skt.	Vajracchedikā-prajñāpāramitā-sūtra	

Vol. No.		Title	T. No.
11-III	*Ch.*	Jên-wang-pan-jo-po-lo-mi-ching (仁王般若波羅蜜經)	245
	Skt.	Kāruṇikārājā-prajñāpāramitā-sūtra (?)	
11-IV	*Ch.*	Pan-jo-po-lo-mi-to-hsing-ching (般若波羅蜜多心經)	251
	Skt.	Prajñāpāramitāhṛdaya-sūtra	
12-I	*Ch.*	Ta-lo-chin-kang-pu-k'ung-chên-shih-san-mo-yeh-ching (大樂金剛不空眞實三麼耶經)	243
	Skt.	Adhyardhaśatikā-prajñāpāramitā-sūtra	
12-II	*Ch.*	Wu-liang-shou-ching (無量壽經)	360
	Skt.	Sukhāvatīvyūha	
	Eng.	The Larger Sutra on Amitāyus (In The Three Pure Land Sutras)	
12-III	*Ch.*	Kuan-wu-liang-shou-fo-ching (觀無量壽佛經)	365
	Skt.	Amitāyurdhyāna-sūtra	
	Eng.	The Sutra on Contemplation of Amitāyus (In The Three Pure Land Sutras)	
12-IV	*Ch.*	A-mi-t'o-ching (阿彌陀經)	366
	Skt.	Sukhāvatīvyūha	
	Eng.	The Smaller Sutra on Amitāyus (In The Three Pure Land Sutras)	
12-V	*Ch.*	Ti-ts'ang-p'u-sa-pên-yüan-ching (地藏菩薩本願經)	412
	Skt.	Kṣitigarbhapraṇidhāna-sūtra (?)	
12-VI	*Ch.*	Yao-shih-liu-li-kuang-ju-lai-pên-yüan-kung-tê-ching (藥師琉璃光如來本願功德經)	450
	Skt.	Bhaiṣajyaguruvaiḍūryaprabhāsapūrva-praṇidhāna-viśeṣavistara	
12-VII	*Ch.*	Mi-lê-hsia-shêng-ch'êng-fo-ching (彌勒下生成佛經)	454
	Skt.	Maitreyavyākaraṇa (?)	
12-VIII	*Ch.*	Wên-shu-shih-li-wên-ching (文殊師利問經)	468
	Skt.	Mañjuśrīparipṛcchā (?)	
13-I	*Ch.*	Miao-fa-lien-hua-ching (妙法蓮華經)	262
	Skt.	Saddharmapuṇḍarīka-sūtra	
	Eng.	The Lotus Sutra	
13-II	*Ch.*	Wu-liang-i-ching (無量義經)	276

Vol. No.		Title	T. No.
13-III	*Ch.*	Kuan-p'u-hsien-p'u-sa-hsing-fa-ching (觀普賢菩薩行法經)	277
14–19	*Ch.*	Ta-fang-kuang-fo-hua-yen-ching (大方廣佛華嚴經)	278
	Skt.	Avataṃsaka-sūtra	
20-I	*Ch.*	Shêng-man-shih-tzŭ-hou-i-ch'eng-ta-fang-pien-fang-kuang-ching (勝鬘師子吼一乘大方便方廣經)	353
	Skt.	Śrīmālādevīsiṃhanāda-sūtra	
20-II	*Ch.*	Chin-kuang-ming-tsui-shêng-wang-ching (金光明最勝王經)	665
	Skt.	Suvarṇaprabhāsa-sūtra	
21–24	*Ch.*	Ta-pan-nieh-p'an-ching (大般涅槃經)	374
	Skt.	Mahāparinirvāṇa-sūtra	
25-I	*Ch.*	Fo-ch'ui-pan-nieh-p'an-liao-shuo-chiao-chieh-ching (佛垂般涅槃略説教誡經)	389
25-II	*Ch.*	Pan-chou-san-mei-ching (般舟三昧經)	418
	Skt.	Pratyutpannabuddhasammukhāvasthitasamādhi-sūtra	
	Eng.	The Pratyutpanna Samādhi Sutra	
25-III	*Ch.*	Shou-lêng-yen-san-mei-ching (首楞嚴三昧經)	642
	Skt.	Śūraṅgamasamādhi-sūtra	
	Eng.	The Śūraṅgama Samādhi Sutra	
25-IV	*Ch.*	Chieh-shên-mi-ching (解深密經)	676
	Skt.	Saṃdhinirmocana-sūtra	
25-V	*Ch.*	Yü-lan-p'ên-ching (盂蘭盆經)	685
	Skt.	Ullambana-sūtra (?)	
25-VI	*Ch.*	Ssŭ-shih-êrh-chang-ching (四十二章經)	784
26-I	*Ch.*	Wei-mo-chieh-so-shuo-ching (維摩詰所説經)	475
	Skt.	Vimalakīrtinirdeśa-sūtra	
26-II	*Ch.*	Yüeh-shang-nü-ching (月上女經)	480
	Skt.	Candrottarādārikāparipṛcchā	
26-III	*Ch.*	Tso-ch'an-san-mei-ching (坐禪三昧經)	614

Vol. No.		Title	*T.* No.
26-IV	*Ch.* *Skt.*	Ta-mo-to-lo-ch'an-ching (達磨多羅禪經) Yogācārabhūmi-sūtra (?)	618
27	*Ch.* *Skt.*	Yüeh-têng-san-mei-ching (月燈三昧經) Samādhirājacandrapradīpa-sūtra	639
28	*Ch.* *Skt.*	Ju-lêng-ch'ieh-ching (入楞伽經) Laṅkāvatāra-sūtra	671
29-I	*Ch.*	Ta-fang-kuang-yüan-chio-hsiu-to-lo-liao-i-ching (大方廣圓覺修多羅了義經)	842
29-II	*Ch.* *Skt.*	Su-hsi-ti-chieh-lo-ching (蘇悉地羯囉經) Susiddhikaramahātantrasādhanopāyika-paṭala	893
29-III	*Ch.* *Skt.*	Mo-têng-ch'ieh-ching (摩登伽經) Mātaṅgī-sūtra (?)	1300
30-I	*Ch.* *Skt.*	Ta-p'i-lu-chê-na-chêng-fo-shên-pien-chia-ch'ih-ching (大毘盧遮那成佛神變加持經) Mahāvairocanābhisambodhivikurvitādhiṣṭhāna-vaipulyasūtrendrarāja-nāma-dharmaparyāya	848
30-II	*Ch.* *Skt.*	Ching-kang-ting-i-ch'ieh-ju-lai-chên-shih-shê-ta-ch'eng-hsien-chêng-ta-chiao-wang-ching (金剛頂一切如來眞實攝大乘現證大教王經) Sarvatathāgatatattvasaṃgrahamahāyānābhi-samayamahākalparāja	865
31–35	*Ch.* *Skt.*	Mo-ho-sêng-ch'i-lü (摩訶僧祇律) Mahāsāṃghika-vinaya (?)	1425
36–42	*Ch.* *Skt.*	Ssŭ-fên-lü (四分律) Dharmaguptaka-vinaya (?)	1428
43, 44	*Ch.* *Pāli*	Shan-chien-lü-p'i-p'o-sha (善見律毘婆沙) Samantapāsādikā	1462
45-I	*Ch.* *Skt.*	Fan-wang-ching (梵網經) Brahmajāla-sūtra (?)	1484
45-II	*Ch.* *Skt.*	Yu-p'o-sai-chieh-ching (優婆塞戒經) Upāsakaśīla-sūtra (?)	1488

Vol. No.		Title	*T*. No.
46-I	*Eng.*	The Sutra on Upāsaka Precepts	1519
	Ch.	Miao-fa-lien-hua-ching-yu-po-t'i-shê (妙法蓮華經憂波提舍)	
	Skt.	Saddharmapuṇḍarīka-upadeśa	
46-II	*Ch.*	Fo-ti-ching-lun (佛地經論)	1530
	Skt.	Buddhabhūmisūtra-śāstra (?)	
46-III	*Ch.*	Shê-ta-ch'eng-lun (攝大乘論)	1593
	Skt.	Mahāyānasaṃgraha	
	Eng.	The Summary of the Great Vehicle	
47	*Ch.*	Shih-chu-p'i-p'o-sha-lun (十住毘婆沙論)	1521
	Skt.	Daśabhūmika-vibhāṣā (?)	
48, 49	*Ch.*	A-p'i-ta-mo-chü-shê-lun (阿毘達磨俱舍論)	1558
	Skt.	Abhidharmakośa-bhāṣya	
50–59	*Ch.*	Yü-ch'ieh-shih-ti-lun (瑜伽師地論)	1579
	Skt.	Yogācārabhūmi	
60-I	*Ch.*	Ch'êng-wei-shih-lun (成唯識論)	1585
	Skt.	Vijñaptimātratāsiddhi-śāstra (?)	
60-II	*Ch.*	Wei-shih-san-shih-lun-sung (唯識三十論頌)	1586
	Skt.	Triṃśikā	
60-III	*Ch.*	Wei-shih-êrh-shih-lun (唯識二十論)	1590
	Skt.	Viṃśatikā	
61-I	*Ch.*	Chung-lun (中論)	1564
	Skt.	Madhyamaka-śāstra	
61-II	*Ch.*	Pien-chung-pien-lun (辯中邊論)	1600
	Skt.	Madhyāntavibhāga	
61-III	*Ch.*	Ta-ch'eng-ch'êng-yeh-lun (大乘成業論)	1609
	Skt.	Karmasiddhiprakaraṇa	
61-IV	*Ch.*	Yin-ming-ju-chêng-li-lun (因明入正理論)	1630
	Skt.	Nyāyapraveśa	
61-V	*Ch.*	Chin-kang-chên-lun (金剛針論)	1642
	Skt.	Vajrasūcī	

Vol. No.		Title	T. No.
61-VI	*Ch.*	Chang-so-chih-lun （彰所知論）	1645
62	*Ch.* *Skt.*	Ta-ch'eng-chuang-yen-ching-lun （大乘莊嚴經論） Mahāyānasūtrālaṃkāra	1604
63-I	*Ch.* *Skt.*	Chiu-ching-i-ch'eng-pao-hsing-lun （究竟一乘寶性論） Ratnagotravibhāgamahāyānottaratantra-śāstra	1611
63-II	*Ch.* *Skt.*	P'u-t'i-hsing-ching （菩提行經） Bodhicaryāvatāra	1662
63-III	*Ch.*	Chin-kang-ting-yü-ch'ieh-chung-fa-a-nou-to-lo-san-miao-san-p'u-t'i-hsin-lun （金剛頂瑜伽中發阿耨多羅三藐三菩提心論）	1665
63-IV	*Ch.* *Skt.*	Ta-ch'eng-ch'i-hsin-lun （大乘起信論） Mahāyānaśraddhotpāda-śāstra (?)	1666
63-V	*Ch.* *Pāli*	Na-hsien-pi-ch'iu-ching （那先比丘經） Milindapañhā	1670
64	*Ch.* *Skt.*	Ta-ch'eng-chi-p'u-sa-hsüeh-lun （大乘集菩薩學論） Śikṣāsamuccaya	1636
65	*Ch.*	Shih-mo-ho-yen-lun （釋摩訶衍論）	1688
66-I	*Ch.*	Pan-jo-po-lo-mi-to-hsin-ching-yu-tsan （般若波羅蜜多心經幽賛）	1710
66-II	*Ch.*	Kuan-wu-liang-shou-fo-ching-shu （觀無量壽佛經疏）	1753
66-III	*Ch.*	San-lun-hsüan-i （三論玄義）	1852
66-IV	*Ch.*	Chao-lun （肇論）	1858
67, 68	*Ch.*	Miao-fa-lien-hua-ching-hsüan-i （妙法蓮華經玄義）	1716
69	*Ch.*	Ta-ch'eng-hsüan-lun （大乘玄論）	1853
70-I	*Ch.*	Hua-yen-i-ch'eng-chiao-i-fên-ch'i-chang （華嚴一乘教義分齊章）	1866

Vol. No.		Title	*T.* No.
70-II	*Ch.*	Yüan-jên-lun （原人論）	1886
70-III	*Ch.*	Hsiu-hsi-chih-kuan-tso-ch'an-fa-yao （修習止觀坐禪法要）	1915
70-IV	*Ch.*	T'ien-t'ai-ssŭ-chiao-i （天台四教儀）	1931
71, 72	*Ch.*	Mo-ho-chih-kuan （摩訶止觀）	1911
73-I	*Ch.*	Kuo-ch'ing-pai-lu （國清百録）	1934
73-II	*Ch.*	Liu-tsu-ta-shih-fa-pao-t'an-ching （六祖大師法寶壇經）	2008
73-III	*Ch.*	Huang-po-shan-tuan-chi-ch'an-shih-ch'uan-hsin-fa-yao （黄檗山斷際禪師傳心法要）	2012A
73-IV	*Ch.*	Yung-chia-chêng-tao-ko （永嘉證道歌）	2014
74-I	*Ch.*	Chên-chou-lin-chi-hui-chao-ch'an-shih-wu-lu （鎭州臨濟慧照禪師語録）	1985
	Eng.	The Recorded Sayings of Linji (In Three Chan Classics)	
74-II	*Ch.*	Wu-mên-kuan （無門關）	2005
	Eng.	Wumen's Gate (In Three Chan Classics)	
74-III	*Ch.*	Hsin-hsin-ming （信心銘）	2010
	Eng.	The Faith-Mind Maxim (In Three Chan Classics)	
74-IV	*Ch.*	Ch'ih-hsiu-pai-chang-ch'ing-kuei （勅修百丈清規）	2025
75	*Ch.*	Fo-kuo-yüan-wu-ch'an-shih-pi-yen-lu （佛果圜悟禪師碧巖録）	2003
	Eng.	The Blue Cliff Record	
76-I	*Ch.*	I-pu-tsung-lun-lun （異部宗輪論）	2031
	Skt.	Samayabhedoparacanacakra	
76-II	*Ch.*	A-yü-wang-ching （阿育王經）	2043
	Skt.	Aśokarāja-sūtra (?)	
	Eng.	The Biographical Scripture of King Aśoka	
76-III	*Ch.*	Ma-ming-p'u-sa-ch'uan （馬鳴菩薩傳）	2046

Vol. No.		Title	T. No.
76-IV	*Ch.*	Lung-shu-p'u-sa-ch'uan (龍樹菩薩傳)	2047
76-V	*Ch.*	P'o-sou-p'an-tou-fa-shih-ch'uan (婆藪槃豆法師傳)	2049
76-VI	*Ch.*	Pi-ch'iu-ni-ch'uan (比丘尼傳)	2063
76-VII	*Ch.*	Kao-sêng-fa-hsien-ch'uan (高僧法顯傳)	2085
76-VIII	*Ch.*	Yu-fang-chi-ch'ao: T'ang-ta-ho-shang-tung-chêng-ch'uan (遊方記抄: 唐大和上東征傳)	2089-(7)
	Eng.	The Great Tang Dynasty Record of the Western Regions	
77	*Ch.*	Ta-t'ang-ta-tz'ŭ-ên-ssŭ-san-ts'ang-fa-shih-ch'uan (大唐大慈恩寺三藏法師傳)	2053
	Eng.	A Biography of the Tripiṭaka Master of the Great Ci'en Monastery of the Great Tang Dynasty	
78	*Ch.*	Kao-sêng-ch'uan (高僧傳)	2059
79	*Ch.*	Ta-t'ang-hsi-yü-chi (大唐西域記)	2087
80	*Ch.*	Hung-ming-chi (弘明集)	2102
81–92	*Ch.*	Fa-yüan-chu-lin (法苑珠林)	2122
93-I	*Ch.*	Nan-hai-chi-kuei-nei-fa-ch'uan (南海寄歸内法傳)	2125
93-II	*Ch.*	Fan-yü-tsa-ming (梵語雑名)	2135
94-I	*Jp.*	Shō-man-gyō-gi-sho (勝鬘經義疏)	2185
94-II	*Jp.*	Yui-ma-kyō-gi-sho (維摩經義疏)	2186
95	*Jp.*	Hok-ke-gi-sho (法華義疏)	2187
96-I	*Jp.*	Han-nya-shin-gyō-hi-ken (般若心經秘鍵)	2203
96-II	*Jp.*	Dao-jō-hos-sō-ken-jin-shō (大乘法相研神章)	2309
96-III	*Jp.*	Kan-jin-kaku-mu-shō (觀心覺夢鈔)	2312
97-I	*Jp.*	Ris-shū-kō-yō (律宗綱要)	2348
	Eng.	The Essentials of the Vinaya Tradition	

Vol. No.		Title	*T.* No.
97-II	*Jp.*	Ten-dai-hok-ke-shū-gi-shū （天台法華宗義集）	2366
	Eng.	The Collected Teachings of the Tendai Lotus School	
97-III	*Jp.*	Ken-kai-ron （顯戒論）	2376
97-IV	*Jp.*	San-ge-gaku-shō-shiki （山家學生式）	2377
98-I	*Jp.*	Hi-zō-hō-yaku （秘藏寶鑰）	2426
98-II	*Jp.*	Ben-ken-mitsu-ni-kyō-ron （辨顯密二教論）	2427
98-III	*Jp.*	Soku-shin-jō-butsu-gi （即身成佛義）	2428
98-IV	*Jp.*	Shō-ji-jis-sō-gi （聲字實相義）	2429
98-V	*Jp.*	Un-ji-gi （吽字義）	2430
98-VI	*Jp.*	Go-rin-ku-ji-myō-hi-mitsu-shaku （五輪九字明秘密釋）	2514
98-VII	*Jp.*	Mitsu-gon-in-hotsu-ro-san-ge-mon （密嚴院發露懺悔文）	2527
98-VIII	*Jp.*	Kō-zen-go-koku-ron （興禪護國論）	2543
98-IX	*Jp.*	Fu-kan-za-zen-gi （普勧坐禪儀）	2580
99–103	*Jp.*	Shō-bō-gen-zō （正法眼藏）	2582
104-I	*Jp.*	Za-zen-yō-jin-ki （坐禪用心記）	2586
104-II	*Jp.*	Sen-chaku-hon-gan-nen-butsu-shū （選擇本願念佛集）	2608
	Eng.	Senchaku Hongan Nembutsu Shū	
104-III	*Jp.*	Ris-shō-an-koku-ron （立正安國論）	2688
104-IV	*Jp.*	Kai-moku-shō （開目抄）	2689
104-V	*Jp.*	Kan-jin-hon-zon-shō （觀心本尊抄）	2692
104-VI	*Ch.*	Fu-mu-ên-chung-ching （父母恩重經）	2887
105-I	*Jp.*	Ken-jō-do-shin-jitsu-kyō-gyō-shō-mon-rui （顯淨土眞實教行証文類）	2646

Vol. No.		Title	T. No.
105-II	*Jp.*	Tan-ni-shō (歎異抄)	2661
	Eng.	Tannishō: Passages Deploring Deviations of Faith	
106-I	*Jp.*	Ren-nyo-shō-nin-o-fumi (蓮如上人御文)	2668
	Eng.	Rennyo Shōnin Ofumi: The Letters of Rennyo	
106-II	*Jp.*	Ō-jō-yō-shū (往生要集)	2682
107-I	*Jp.*	Has-shū-kō-yō (八宗綱要)	蔵外
	Eng.	The Essentials of the Eight Traditions	
107-II	*Jp.*	San-gō-shī-ki (三教指帰)	蔵外
107-III	*Jp.*	Map-pō-tō-myō-ki (末法燈明記)	蔵外
	Eng.	The Candle of the Latter Dharma	
107-IV	*Jp.*	Jū-shichi-jō-ken-pō (十七條憲法)	蔵外